SECTORAL RESPONSES TO A NEW WORLD ORDER: THE EUROPEAN UNION AND ITS POLICIES

Edited by Péter Balázs

T0346380

SECTORAL RESPONSES TO A NEW WORLD ORDER: THE EUROPEAN UNION AND ITS POLICIES

Edited by Péter Balázs

Center for EU Enlargement Studies

2014

©2014 by Center for EU Enlargement Studies
Published in 2014 by
Center for EU Enlargement Studies

Distributed by
Central European University Press

An imprint of the Central European University Limited Liability Company
Nádor utca 11, H-1051 Budapest, Hungary
Tel: +36-1-327-3138 or 327-3000
Fax: +36-1-327-3183
E-mail: ceupress@ceu.hu
Website: www.ceupress.com

Ábel Mészáros
224 West 57th Street, New York 10019, USA
Tel.: +1-732-763-8816
E-mail: meszarosa@ceu.hu

ISBN 978-963-89822-6-1

This publication was sponsored by the Hungarian Scientific Research Fund (OTKA) under the project "The changing world order and its implications for the wider Europe" (OTKA 84079).

Library of Congress Control Number: 2014956056

Printed in Hungary

TABLE OF CONTENTS

INTRODUCTION

PÉTER BALÁZS

With the Lisbon Treaty, the European Union (EU) set out to transform itself into an entity in world politics. Drawing strength from the Union's *sui generis* nature as a unique economic and political project, its member states sought to make the EU a more influential global actor. Enthusiasm seemed well-founded: the EU was one of the economic power centers of the world, its member states were on the path of further integration (a path that involved foreign and security policy), and the states of Central and Eastern Europe, performing a deep systemic change, were on the verge of completing their "return to Europe." This widespread euphemism was widely visible in documents such as the 2003 security strategy "A Secure Europe," or in the words of its high representative for foreign affairs, Javier Solana, that the claim that the European Union is a global player is "not an aspiration but a statement of fact." (Solana 2005)

Indeed, by the second half of the 2000s, the EU had become a regional stabilizer and had expanded its influence both in the wider Europe and globally. This role thus came with its own discourse defining the EU as a "force of good," as a "peacebuilder," thereby legitimizing the Union's task in global politics. (Aggestam, 2008) In fact, the EU acted as a normative anchor for its new member states and for Western Balkan countries eager to join the Union, and sought to bring closer its Eastern neighbors through the Eastern Partnership instrument. Close cooperation bringing economic benefit, with the vague promise of eventual membership, seemed to be sufficient to provide leverage over the neighborhood. During those years, the EU also expanded the number of its missions globally, and contributed to defining what counts as normal in world politics. The EU made serious efforts to become a key institutional element of the transatlantic community besides the North Atlantic Treaty Organization (NATO). Through its considerable presence in world trade, the EU also strived to appear along the United States (US) as a coercive authority in global affairs, such as in the Middle East peace process or the negotiations about Iran's nuclear program.

However, in the past few years, the changing international order, the decrease in European competitiveness and economic output, and a number of internal institutional compromises, have begun to challenge the EU's ability to perform its role as a global actor, indeed even its role as a regional stabilizer. The repercussions of the global financial crisis in the Eurozone, the ongoing military conflict in Ukraine, the US's continuing pivot to Asia all hamper the Union's ability to act. Its magnetism too weakened: partner countries now left without a clear path to accession appear to be much more opportunistic when it comes to their EU relations than were the enthusiastic post-communistic states of the 2004 enlargement wave.

But the problems at hand are not only external. The EU seems to be sluggish in responding to new challenges due to an institutional structure that is at the same time far too sophisticated and slow to keep the pace of change. In fact, whether the Union will continue on its way towards closer integration or move back towards intergovernmentalism is not an internal issue. Many of the policies that are key to responding to the needs of a new world order, and to maintaining stability in a wider Europe, fall under various competences: some involve strong European capabilities; others, strong nation states. Coordination is essential, but it cannot work without a political vision.

The present book is a continuation of a three-year joint research effort by Hungarian scholars that set out an impossible task: to survey both the challenges that the EU as a global actor has been facing since the 2008 financial crisis, and the policy responses it gives (or should give) to these challenges. As has been visible in recent years, all these issues are in constant flux, and the EU itself also presents "a moving target" that is difficult to pin down. Therefore, instead of offering ready-made answers or a definite explanation for the turmoil Europe is now in, the authors of this volume instead point readers towards the pivotal policy questions that we need to focus on in the near future as analysts, as policy-makers and also as European citizens.

Due to the diversity of issues that represent the challenge side of the equation, the topics here necessarily needed to be narrowed down. Accordingly, the chapters assess key areas of European policy such as internal institutional reform, foreign policy, security policy, trade, energy security and migration. The contributors believe that this selection offers a non-exclusive list of policy areas that the EU can use to shape both itself and its environment in a way that is favorable for a stable and prosperous "wider Europe."

Bibliography

Aggestam, L. (2008). Introduction: ethical power Europe? *International Affairs*. 84(1), 1-10.
Solana, J. (2005). Speech on "Shaping an Effective EU Foreign Policy." Brussels: Konrad Adenauer Foundation.

SECTORAL POLICIES OF THE EUROPEAN UNION

The complex system of European integration has developed in three different dimensions: first, in the legal and institutional domain; second, in the area of sectoral policies; and third, through the enlargement of the European Union (EU) with new member states. The results of these three parallel processes altogether reflect the general state of integration. Without doubt, strong interaction exists among the three dimensions; however, their individual progress, stagnation or even their regression can also be the result of processes that are independent of each other. The three domains attract various degrees of attention from different groups of stakeholders. The development of legal and institutional foundations is a matter concerning first and foremost the member states, as this dimension can mostly be enriched by transferring competences from them to the Union level. The progress made in sectoral policy areas is important for the EU member states participating in the common governance of the EU, but these processes have a growing impact on the EU's relations with third countries as well. The accession of new states affects and interests the EU member countries, the current and prospective candidates and the wider outside world, as it changes the scope, the influence and the motivations of the EU as one of the biggest international actors.

The interest of third countries arose more from the process of EU enlargement than from the internal sectoral development of integration. During the past half century developing integration caused the membership of the EU to increase to more than four times its original size. The accession of new states happens through a highly visible and greatly politicized process which is accompanied by such notable moments as the decision to apply for EU membership in the respective countries, the submission of the application for membership and its reception at the EU level, the opening of the negotiations and the closure of the various chapters, the transposition of the EU's legal and institutional system into the candidates' domestic legal order, the reactions of the domestic and wider European public, etc.

The re-occurring reforms of the EU's legal and institutional foundations also receive greater attention than the conduct of its sectoral policies. The ever newer versions of the basic treaty and its accompanying documents, together with the functioning competences and the changing structure of the institutions, are the results of serious political bargaining among member states within the Union. This continuous reform process is called, popularly and superficially, "deepening" and is put in parallel with the enlargement of the Union to new member states, which is sometimes referred to as "widening." However, this latter term should be reserved to the third, less spectacular dimension of the European integration's development, namely the extension of the European model of two-level governance to a growing number of sectoral policy areas. In reality, this "widening" of the integration is an additional aspect of both the "deepening" and the "enlarging" of the EU. While the legal and institutional dimensions reflect the intensity of cooperation among states, the growing number of sectoral policy areas indicates that member states consider the delegation to the European Union of competences in more and more sectors to be desirable (thus, the "widening" of the scope of common governance), and the strengthening of their cooperation in these domains to be advantageous (hence, the "deepening" of the integration through stronger European coordination). These developments in the scope and depth of common sectoral governance often necessitate institutional changes, which in turn can result in significant re-arrangements in the complex system of governance of the European Union.

The smooth and successful functioning of the EU to a large extent depends– just as with any organization –on whether its institutions can perform their tasks and can cooperate with each other efficiently. Such cooperation can be measured in an appropriate manner within and among the sectors their activities encompass. In this regard, the vertical and horizontal coherence of sectoral policy coordination in the European Union is of particular importance due to its unique two-level structure of governance. While the vertical coherence determines how well member states' governing bodies and EU institutions correspond and connect to each other, the state of the horizontal coherence predicts how well common trans-sectoral governance can function on the community level between and among the EU institutions. The internal functioning of the organization, as influenced by these two factors, also determines whether the European Union will be able to appear as a leading power on the international stage. Therefore, we argue that a prerequisite for the European Union to be able to assume a strong role in the world is the efficiency and harmonious functioning of its own institutions through the vertical and horizontal coherence of the sectoral policies.

In this chapter, we analyze the development of the integration of the EU in the domain of sectoral policies by focusing on the structure of EU institutions as well as on their interrelations in implementing common governance. We seek to examine, more particularly, how the institutional frameworks of the European Union allow for cooperation and coordination in areas of common sectoral governance and whether they make possible a smooth functioning of sectoral coordination through an appropriate level of vertical and horizontal coherence of the institutions. To this aim, the chapter will progress as follows: after a brief introduction into the development of the European integration's sectoral competences, we will discuss in detail how these competences are divided between EU institutions and member states under the most elaborate basic treaty to date, the Treaty of Lisbon (including the Treaty on European Union and the Treaty on the Functioning of the European Union). We will then analyze in depth how each of the three main EU institutions, the Council of Ministers, the European Commission and the European Parliament (EP), cover the sectoral policy areas and how these match a set of governmental functions we identify as core areas of governance based on national experience in EU member states. Finally, we will conclude with an overall analysis that will shed light on whether the current sectoral task distribution in the main EU institutions meets the necessary prerequisites of successful sectoral governance, that is, whether a strong level of both vertical and horizontal coherence is present.

Sectoral cooperation in Europe

The European Economic Community (EEC) was launched in 1957 by the Treaty of Rome with the aim of common governance in only three sectoral policy areas: commerce, agriculture and transport. The common commercial policy (CCP) and the common agricultural policy (CAP) were built on fairly precisely defined aims and well developed toolkits, while the third area, the common transport policy, was only an improvised sketch based on some premature ideas in the Treaty of Rome. The common commercial policy was born as the direct spin-off of the customs union of the six founding countries, Belgium, France, West Germany, Italy, Luxemburg and the Netherlands. It was based on the regulatory system of the General Agreement on Tariffs and Trade (GATT), implemented and further developed in accordance with the main characteristics of the EEC. The common agricultural policy combined the aim of maintaining the competitiveness of the agricultural sector in a highly industrialized society, with the goals and tools of self-sufficiency typical of war economies. Under the conditions of the Cold War, the CAP was rich in elements characteristic of planned economies. Both of these sectoral policies reflected defensive efforts that fitted into the context of the 1950s. Nevertheless, common governance in these two policy areas was not only guided by security concerns but also served to protect the common market of the six founding states from external competition embodied both by developed partners such as the United States, and by countries such as Japan or the planned economies of the Comecon which, at this time, posed a threat to the common market through potential dumping.

At this point, competences within the EEC were either held at the community or at the member state level, creating a clear-cut bipolar division between the two levels of governance. Moreover, in the first decade of the integration, policy making remained predominantly at the level of member states even in those areas where the EEC treaty allowed for the development of community-level policies. Only from the late 1960s did the Communities start to legislate and develop policy on a wider range of sectors, going well beyond the initial core community competences. This process blurred the pre-existing dividing line and created a spectrum of shared competences where both member states and the Communities legislated. (Pollack, 2000, pp. 521-523)

Enlargements, with the regular arrival of new member states, followed a fundamentally different path of integration than the incorporation of various sectoral policies into the domain of common governance. The ultimate goal of enlargement was already set in the Treaty of Rome (Article 237) which stated that "any European State may apply to become a member of the Community." This principle was laid down even though at the time of this declaration Europe was still divided by the Iron Curtain and the interpretation of the geographic term "any European State" remained blurry. Nonetheless, with regards to the geographic enlargement of the integration, a clear *finalité politique* existed from the beginning. This was not the case in the domain of sectoral integration where the Treaty did not set future goals.

Nevertheless, European integration theorists did outline certain paths they thought the Communities would follow. While enlargement is often seen through the federalist or confederalist idea of uniting the states of Europe, the progress in the dimension of common sectoral governance is explained by the more concrete neo-functionalist concepts.[1] Scholars of neo-functionalism explain the dynamics of political integration through the shifting loyalties of political actors from the national to the supranational level and through the spillover hypothesis. In the view of the spiritual founder of this theory, Ernst Haas, the participating actors are persuaded, through the process of political integration, to shift their loyalties and political activities toward the center of the integration that develops jurisdiction over the national level. The result is a new political community superimposed on the pre-existing ones (Haas, 1958, p. 16), but with the participation of the earlier national political actors whose shifting loyalties would make them the new drivers of the integration process. Additionally, according to the neo-functionalist spillover hypothesis, the common governance of selected sectors would inevitably lead to a demand for the integration of further, connected governmental activities. The spillover effect results in more and more sectors being integrated into the governing mechanisms of the new political community, partly to release the technical, functional pressures arising from the integration of previous sectors, and partly to optimize the effectiveness of governance.

The neo-functionalist theoretical model, for a while, seemed to be vindicated by the practice of European integration. In fact, the circle of sectoral policies under common governance gradually started to expand from the late 1960s and throughout the 1970s. The long-term consequence of the spillover mechanism would have been the continuous decrease of member state competences paralleled by the increase of community powers. It seemed that in the framework of the integration a conscious transfer of competences would take place through which the member states lose increasing parts of their sovereignty, which in turn end up with the new political and economic community. (See also Benz & Zimmer, 2010)

Practice, however, revealed two important circumstances. First, it showed that the responsibility of member states' governments did not cease to exist even if the policy area was transferred to the exclusive competence of the community. In other words, community-level governance is built on the active participation of the member states. Well-founded national positions are indispensable for work coordination in the common bodies of the integration, where national stakeholders represent their constituencies. Since the most powerful decision-making EU institution, the Council of Ministers, remained of intergovernmental and not supranational character, the exclusivity of the community competence is to be understood as solely common – i.e. no national decisions are made in the given sector. This means that such decisions are made with the participation of the member states even if decision making is elevated to the higher, community level of governance. Accordingly, member states have also maintained – and in several cases even strengthened – ministries responsible for sectors that belong to exclusive community competence.

---

1   Federalist and neo-functionalist approaches are often contrasted, and the dichotomy they entail is most visible through the legal and institutional development of the integration, where the federalist political program of the unification of Europe was often antagonized by the doctrine of member state sovereignty, in turn suitably supported by the pragmatic neo-functionalist approach which only supports common governance in areas where it is in the interest of the member states. The concrete solutions appearing in the modifications of the basic treaty over time reflected the compromises of the two approaches favoring first one, then the other. The latest steps that evolved in the Lisbon Treaty, for example, signal an obvious divergence from the goal of federalism.

It has to be underlined that member state positions are strongly needed on these areas. As integration developed, the division between national and community competence gradually became blurred in several sectoral areas newly entering the sphere of common governance. It was generally accepted that the community and its member states jointly exercise the competences and that their two-level governance moves in reality on a spectrum between community and national competences. (See the categorization in Schmitter, 1996, pp. 125-126) In the beginning, these "mixed" competences were mostly regarded as temporary categories, as activity areas where political powers had started to move from the national toward the community level, but where this transition was not yet complete. Later, however, it showed that the member states are quite comfortable with such undefined, in-between competences, and hence the temporary concept of "mixed" or "shared" competences was consolidated and took legal shape. In fact, shared competences today represent the major share within all the various categories.

Second, it became clear that the legal transfer or the exclusive or shared competences to the community is a necessary, but not sufficient requirement to exercise control over the given sector on the community level. General prerequisites of policy making also have to be established on the community level. First of all, common policy objectives should be discussed, defined and agreed upon at the EU Ministerial Council level. Furthermore, instruments and institutions of implementation (human and financial resources) must be established. Finally, the legal and institutional framework and conditions of execution must be created at the EU level. In this policy making and policy enforcing process, the member states play the decisive role, even if the competences are entirely transferred to the EU, but the key elements of the policy cycle have to be shaped for the implementation of the common policy.

Sectoral integration under the Lisbon Treaty

The incorporation of newer policy areas into the system of integrated governance seemed by the early 2000s to have reached a limit as the member states' readiness to "deepen and widen" the integration came to its temporary maximum, along with the technical feasibility of the two-level governance. However, the number of integrated sectors grew still further as several of them have been subdivided in parallel with the last enlargement rounds of the European Union. After the adoption of the Lisbon Treaty we arrived to about 25 sectors that are listed under exclusive or shared EU competence, as well as under supporting competence – a new category introduced by the Lisbon Treaty. In order to evaluate the actual depth of the European Union's sectoral integration, in the following section we will discuss the current division of EU competences, will examine how the sectoral structure of EU institutions corresponds to this division, and will contrast this with the typical governmental functions of a European state. The goal of this exercise is, first of all, to see how the two levels of European governance correspond to each other. This vertical analysis will serve as the foundation to examine whether the sectoral governance of the EU helps the smooth implementation of the policy cycle in the European Union.

The current division of competencies concerning sectoral cooperation is laid out in the Treaty on the Functioning of the European Union (TFEU) in Articles 3, 4 and 6. Article 3 of the TFEU states that *"the Union shall have exclusive competence in the following areas:*

(a) customs union;[2]
(b) the establishing of the competition rules necessary for the functioning of the internal market;
(c) monetary policy for the Member States whose currency is the euro;
(d) the conservation of marine biological resources under the common fisheries policy;
(e) common commercial policy."

As explained before, the exclusive EU competence does not mean the exclusion of the member states *per se* from the integrated decision-making process concerning the given sector, even if all decisions are made and legislation is adopted at the fora and with the inclusion of the EU institutions. This means that the member states cannot legislate in these areas on their own; they can only implement the common European regulations.

Comparing the above list to the original dispositions of the Treaty of Rome, we see that only two areas (monetary policy and the conservation of marine biological resources) have entered the circle of exclusive competences since then. The inclusion of both areas can be explained by the spill-over hypothesis in the sense that the member states started to cooperate in new policy areas in order to ensure that the goals they previously had set in the original sectors of common governance are met (Schmitter, 1969, p. 162) – in this case, in the field of competition and agriculture-fisheries respectively. Both of these areas were closely related to the two fundamental common policies – the Common Commercial Policy and the Common Agricultural Policy – based on exclusive EU competences. In other obvious cases of the spill-over effect, such as for transport, energy, or environment, the member states opted for the more comfortable system of shared competences, where they could preserve partial direct control over the integrated governance activities.

Article 4 (TFEU) lists the areas of shared competence between the Union and the member states as follows:

"(a) internal market;
(b) social policy, for the aspects defined in this Treaty;
(c) economic, social and territorial cohesion;
(d) agriculture and fisheries, excluding the conservation of marine biological resources;
(e) environment;
(f) consumer protection;
(g) transport;
(h) trans-European networks;
(i) energy;
(j) area of freedom, security and justice;
(k) common safety concerns in public health matters, for the aspects defined in this Treaty."

Additionally, in the field of *research, technological development and space*, as well as *development cooperation and humanitarian aid*, the Union received competence to carry out activities, define and implement programs or develop common policies, but in these two spheres the EU competence does not restrict the competence of the member states to matters where there is no community legislation, as it does in general in sectors of shared competence (Article 4 TFEU, points 3 and 4).

---

2   The customs union between the six founding states served as a technical and political basis for the development of the three areas of common governance in the Treaty of Rome.

The Lisbon Treaty also introduced a new type of EU power, the so-called supporting competence, which gives supplementary roles to the European Union, even if the areas under this category are governed by the EU member states on the national level. The EU does not have legislative powers here, but the new category resembles the practice of the open method of coordination (OMC).[3] The OMC offered a tool that has been used in sectors where the EU did not have powers, but where the EU institutions and member states found it useful to harmonize their actions. According to Article 6 (TFEU), the following sectors fall under this competence:

"(a) protection and improvement of human health;
(b) industry;
(c) culture;
(d) tourism;
(e) education, vocational training, youth and sport;
(f) civil protection;
(g) administrative cooperation."

The foreign and security policy of the member states does not belong to either of the above three categories, as the Common Foreign and Security Policy of the European Union is regulated as an intergovernmental policy under Article 24 of the TFEU. Furthermore, there are other policy areas, such as defense, which remain in the exclusive competence of the member states.[4]

Based on the cumulated list of all the exclusive, shared and supporting competences as laid down in the Lisbon Treaty, the operation of common consultative and decision-making bodies as well as the development of common sectoral policies can be regarded as legitimate on the European level in the areas listed in Table 1.[5] We have aligned the individual sectors with those governmental functions that are common to EU member states in general. Based on our research, the 20 sectors listed in Table 1 correspond to the usual profiles of the ministries of a well-structured, democratic and transparent national government.[6] Certain sectors listed under the TFEU have not been considered here as a separate function (e.g. "trans-European networks," "culture," "civil protection," "protection and improvement of

3   The Open Method of Coordination was invented and introduced by the European Council of Lisbon in March 2000, targeting a quantitative leap in the EU's world-wide competitiveness.
4   As an additional category, it should be mentioned that under Article 5 of the TFEU the European Union has certain special coordinating competences as well, which are not usually listed among the general threefold division of competences in the literature. This means that the EU can set targets and guidelines for the EU as a whole and for its member states in the sphere of economic policy, and that in the sector of employment and social policy it should ensure that member states coordinate their policies. They, however, have the authority to govern in these sectors. This new type of competence appeared first in relation to the EU's competitiveness program, the Lisbon Strategy in 2010, the implementation of which clearly belonged to the member states, but where the EU already had coordinator roles.
5   Note that the areas of coordinating competences have not been included in the list.
6   It should be mentioned, however, that all member states have a different governmental structure and the governments vary significantly in size. On the larger end we find France (before 2014) and Sweden with 23 and 25 ministers respectively, while Malta and Hungary take the lead among the smallest governments with 8 ministers each.

human health" as well as "common safety concerns in public health matters") because they are understood to be under a broader sector (transport, education, internal affairs and health respectively). Some sectors that appear on the European level cannot be directly translated into a national function, as they belong to the integrated level of governance functions (e.g. administrative cooperation); therefore we omitted those as well. Finally, defense does not appear in the table because this sector comes solely under member state competence and does not have directly corresponding EU-level bodies, and as such cannot be considered for our analysis.

Table 1. National governmental functions and EU competences

Governmental functions – policy sectors		
Exclusive EU competences	**Shared EU competences**	**Supporting EU competences**
External trade Competition policy	Home affairs Justice Development cooperation Financial and monetary policy Economic, social and territorial cohesion Internal market Consumer protection Agriculture and fisheries Environment Transport and telecommunication Energy Research and development Public health	Industry Tourism Education and vocational training Social policy
Foreign affairs		

Source: Own compilation.

Table 1 (above) groups the governmental functions under the three types of EU competences according to Articles 3, 4 and 6 of the TFEU. Our next question is how the EU institutions' internal structure supports the common exercise of these governmental functions, in line with the current delimitations of competences. To examine this, we take the approach of a comparative structural analysis of the EU Council of Ministers, the European Commission and the European Parliament and we explore the requirements and effectiveness of their mutual cooperation from the angle of sectoral governance.

The Council of the European Union

Bearing a strong intergovernmental character, the Council of the European Union represents the member states of the Union by bringing together their ministers in various council configurations. The Council legislates in various sectoral areas (in close cooperation with the European Parliament), coordinates the economic policies of the member states in order to meet common targets, and decides on actions to be taken and agreements to be signed on the international stage. The Council of the EU concentrates the areas of common governance in ten highly concise sectoral configurations. (See Table 2) One of these is the General

Affairs Council, which plays a predominantly technical role in the internal policy making of the EU; this formation is not included in Table 2 as it does not perform sectoral activities. Its main task is the preparation of the work of the European Council, the institutionalized forum of the member states' heads of states or governments that meets at least four times a year and holds frequent informal meetings. The remaining configurations differ in the scope and frequency of thei r activities: some cover one single governmental function, while others deal with multiple tasks, sometimes embracing a fairly diverse spectrum.

Table 2. National governmental functions and the Council of the European Union

Governmental functions	Configurations of the Council of the European Union
Home affairs	Justice and Home Affairs Council
Justice	
Foreign affairs	Foreign Affairs Council
External trade	
Development cooperation	
Financial and monetary policy	Economic and Financial Affairs Council
Economic, social and territorial cohesion	
Competition policy	
Agriculture and fisheries	Agriculture and Fisheries Council
Environment	Environment Council
Transport and telecommunication	Transport, Telecommunications and Energy Council
Energy	
Social policy	Employment, Social Policy, Health and Consumer Affairs Council
Public health	
Consumer protection	
Internal market	Competitiveness Council
Research and development	
Industry	
Education and vocational training	Education, Youth, Culture and Sport Council

Source: Own compilation.

One of the reasons for the relatively low potential efficiency of the Council of the European Union is to be found in the insufficiency of both its vertical and its horizontal coherence. By vertical coherence, we mean the correspondence of the sectoral divisions of the council formations with the member states' governmental functions. Here we see that government tasks are divided fairly unequally at the integrated EU level and that certain Council formations (e.g. the Competitiveness Council or the Employment, Social Policy, Health and Consumer Affairs Council) cover rather divers sectors. We could expect more vertical coherence between the two levels only if these both sought to meet the prevailing challenges of governance of the time, while simultaneously looking for connections between the national and the community level. For the time being, neither of these preconditions are met.

The member states of the EU form and rearrange their national ministries according to their political traditions and, as mentioned before, the size and structure of the governments varies to a large extent from country to country. The Union does not interfere in these matters at all, not even through recommendations, even though the representatives of the member states' governments in the different council configurations meet frequently and are expected to cooperate. The power-sharing within the country – be it within the governing party or coalition, among the regions or national minorities – is more important for the member states than developing ministry profiles appropriate for international cooperation, and fitting – among others – properly into EU governance structures.

Most member states do have ministers for foreign affairs, finances, agriculture or environment, but such important governmental portfolios as energy, transport, tourism or building industry are usually allotted to the most diverse ministerial configurations due to various internal political considerations. Therefore, vertical coherence between the governing bodies of the member states and of the EU shows a colorful picture: in certain sectors the vertical connection works perfectly (e.g. foreign affairs, monetary policy, agriculture), whereas in other areas we are met with disturbing disarray (e.g. in industry, energy, transport or competitiveness).

The Council of the European Union has several functions similar to those of a government, though it shows a significant difference to national government structures in that EU Council formations bring together the ministers of one single sector (or of a special, limited combination of related sectors). This aspect brings us to the question of the horizontal coherence of European governance, under which we understand the elaboration of trans-sectoral connectedness and the coordination of policies on the level of the integration itself. Since the Council configurations are attended by national government representatives of the same policy area, they strengthen the intra-sectoral coherence within the EU rather than cooperation among different sectors.

Certain council configurations have highly complex profiles (such as transport–telecommunication–energy; employment–social policy–health; education–youth–culture–sport). The idea behind such complexity can be, among others, to use the same forum for discussing different sectoral issues connected to each other.

At the same time, other important sectors and policies are never discussed together institutionally in the EU Council, at least not at the level of ministers. Such is the situation, for example, with the interconnected issues of environment, energy and finance. Attempts were made to hold so-called jumbo council meetings, uniting multiple sectors, but these configurations did not prove viable due to the large number of participants. The main reason for this is that, for the time being, one single sector involves 28 member states' ministers, which is obviously far beyond the ideal dimension of policy-oriented meetings, and the inclusion of two or three related sectors would multiply this figure accordingly. Therefore trans-sectoral aspects, which are constantly present in the governance of any member state through regular government sessions as well as inter-ministerial coordinating mechanisms, and which are one of the main assets of national policy making and executive implementation, are practically absent on sectoral EU Council meetings. Such aspects can appear only at two fora of the Council of the European Union, which both perform very complex tasks: at the Committee of Permanent Representatives (Coreper), which prepares the meetings of the ministers, and at the European Council uniting heads of states or governments. Therefore, we can conclude that the trans-sectoral consistency of the EU's policy seriously lags behind its intra-sectoral cohesion, which hampers the overall effectiveness of EU governance. (Balázs, 2014b)

The European Commission

As opposed to the Council of the EU which expresses the interests of the member states, the European Commission represents the interest of the European Union as an independent entity by drafting and proposing new legal acts to be discussed by the Council and the European Parliament. Moreover, the Commission is responsible for the implementation of common policies and the overall functioning and financing of the EU. The sectoral division of the European Commission is well-reflected by the professional profile of the directorate generals, however for the outside world, including the other EU institutions and the member states, it is the person and the portfolio of the Commissioner that represent the sectoral task divisions in the most visible manner. (See Table 3) We therefore find it advisable to compare the list of governmental functions (Table 1) we established on the basis of EU competence analysis, with the current portfolios of the individual EU Commissioners (of the 2009-2014 European Commission).[7]

Table 3. National governmental functions and the European Commission[8]

Governmental Function	Portfolio	EU Commissioner (2009-2014)
Internal affairs	Home affairs	Cecilia Malmström
Justice	Justice, fundamental rights and citizenship	Viviane Reding
Foreign affairs	High Representative of the Union for foreign affairs and security policy	Catherine Ashton
	Enlargement and neighborhood policy	Stefan Füle
External trade	Trade	Karel De Gucht
Development cooperation	Development	Andris Piebalgs
	International cooperation, humanitarian aid and crisis response	Kristalina Georgieva
Financial and monetary policy	Economic and monetary affairs	Olli Rehn
	Financial programming and budget	Janusz Lewandowski
	Taxation and customs union, audit and anti-fraud	Algirdas Semeta
Economic, social and territorial cohesion	Regional policy	Johannes Hahn
Internal market	Internal market and services	Michel Barnier
Consumer protection	Consumer protection	Neven Mimica
Competition policy	Competition	Joaquín Almunia
Industry	Industry and entrepreneurship	Antonio Tajani
Agriculture and fisheries	Agriculture and rural development	Dacian Ciolos
	Maritime affairs and fisherie	Maria Damanaki

---

7   At the time of closing this analysis, the 2009-2014 European Commission is coming out of office. The evaluation of the institutional structure and of their efficiency can be based on the experience acquired with the actual college of European Commissioners. The next, 2014-2019 European Commission is still being formed and neither its internal structure nor the definitions and distribution of the portfolios have been approved by the European Council and the European Parliament.

8   Two members of the Commission are not in Table 3: Vice-President Maroš Ševčovič who is responsible for an internal portfolio: inter-institutional relations and administration; and President José Manuel Barroso who serves as the President of the Commission without a specific portfolio.

Environment	Climate action	*Connie Hedegaard*
	Environment	*Janez Potocnik*
Transport, telecommunication	Transport	*Siim Kallas*
	Digital agenda	*Neelie Kroes*
Tourism		
Energy	Energy	*Günther Oettinger*
Research and development	Research, innovation and science	*Méire Geoghegann-Quinn*
Education and vocational training	Education, culture, multilingualism, youth	*Androulla Vassiliou*
Public health	Health	*Tonio Borg*
Social policy	Employment, social affairs and inclusion	*László Andor*

Source: Own compilation.

Visibly, the portfolios of the Commissioners correspond much more to core national governmental functions than the broader sectoral configurations of the EU Council. Since the Union introduced the "one Commissioner per member state" principle in 2004, the size of the Commission has grown significantly. The advantage of the new set-up is that it is easier to match, from this broader pool, the portfolios with the core functions; therefore the vertical coherence of the policy areas between the two levels of EU governance is definitely better secured than is the case with the Council of the European Union. Nevertheless, the fact that this principle was adopted again reinforces the dominance of the member states in the European policy-making process and in an institution that, according to its formal status, is expected to represent solely the interests of the Union.

A closer look at Table 3 shows that the 26 sectoral commissioners cover well the 20 governmental functions of Table 1. Five key functions (foreign affairs, development cooperation, financial and monetary policy, agriculture and fisheries, environment) are even subdivided among multiple Commissioners. Such sub-divisions can be evaluated case by case. As to the responsibilities concerning the enlargement and neighborhood policy, it seems reasonable to separate them from the general tasks of foreign and security policy at the EU level. The division of fisheries and the matters of agriculture and rural development is also an understandable decision. However, it seems largely disproportional to give "climate policy" to an individual commissioner instead of incorporating it into environment or energy policy, or to separate the "digital agenda" into an individual portfolio, compared to portfolios where responsibilities span a whole sector, such as with agriculture, energy and others. Entrusting a separate commissioner with the management of the EU budget instead of including it in the portfolio of the commissioner for economic and monetary affairs is again a reasonable decision given the size and importance of the single issue. Nevertheless, it is completely unnecessary to allocate "taxation and customs" into a separate portfolio, just as it is not justified to treat humanitarian aid and international development separately. While keeping such criticism in mind, the task division within the European Commission ensures (with some minor corrections and adjustments) an adequate background for EU-level sectoral governance. This set-up is not far from what we considered to be the optimal arrangement at the beginning of our analysis.

The introduction of the "one Commissioner per member state" principle increased the core staff of the European Commission, hence made a better correspondence possible with the member states' governmental functions; nonetheless, it did not improve the eligibility and selection criteria for the position of the EU Commissioners. Therefore the suitability of the Commissioners should be discussed here, too. In accordance with the current praxis, the nomination of EU Commission members continues to be the privilege of the member states. After the nomination of the members of the European Commission, the member states' governments are not accountable for their suggestion in any way. The procedure therefore raises serious quality concerns as it frees the nominating governments from their political responsibility, which in turn encourages counter-selection. This all the more so as the Commissioners appointed for five years survive – in a political sense – the government that nominated them. The nominees' hearing takes place in the European Parliament, but practice shows that this hearing is a largely formal exercise and is only sufficient for filtering out the extremely incompetent candidates. (Vesnic-Alujevic & Nacarino, 2012) Following the hearing in the European Parliament, the task of the appointment and employment is transferred under the authority of the EU's institutions, that is, by this stage it completely breaks away from the political context that initiated the appointment.

At the moment the very situation is self-contradictory: the Commissioners' nomination continues to depend on the incumbent governments, while the intention is to portray the Commission as a more politicized European institution. With regards to the political composition of the European Commission, the "one Commissioner per member state" principle removed even the slightest traces of political pluralism from the institution. In the previous set-up, since the very beginning of the integration until 2004, the big member states[9] could delegate two Commissioners each, while the small ones could send one each. The two Commissioners of the big member states usually represented the two sides of the domestic political arena – one came from the governing party, the other from the opposition forces. This example motivated the smaller states to exercise the principle of political pluralism over time, first sending the nominee of one side, then that of the other. Similarly, other pluralistic criteria could be met, such as the principle of gender equality between men and women, or the Flemish-Walloon rotation in the case of Belgium.

A new development introduced in 2014 would correspond to the idea of politicizing the Commission: the open election of the Commission President by the majority of the European Parliament from the "top candidates" of the EP party families. With the purposeful interpretation of the Lisbon Treaty, the European Parliament could fill a gap in the vast institutional field of the well-known "democratic deficit:" by transferring the selection of the European Commission's President from the closed rooms of the European Council to a public competition organized and stimulated by the EP. Nevertheless, due to other aspects of the European Union's democracy deficit, this reform will most likely not fully meet the original intention, for three reasons. First, because the "top candidates" were selected from and by the outgoing and not the incoming new EP, which will co-exist and co-operate with the incoming European Commission. Second, because the selection of the other members of the Commission remains in the hands of the national governments, ensuring the perpetuation of the accountability gap mentioned above. And finally, because the European parliamentary majority, unlike in the national parliaments, is not politically accountable to its electorate, which means it can never fail due to bad governance. Therefore, the election of the Commission President will be again a mere formality without political consequences, just as with the hearing of the Commissioners.[10]

---

9   By big member states before 2004, we mean France, Germany, Italy, Spain and the United Kingdom.
10 Forms of democratic deficit in the functioning of the European Union have been discussed in further detail by the author. (See Balázs, 2014b, pp. 240-242)

The European Parliament

The European Parliament provides representation for a third group of actors, the citizens of the European Union. Its main role is to debate and adopt European legislation in cooperation with the Council and to exercise democratic control over the European Commission. Some of the main shortcomings of the European Parliament concerning its legitimacy and its role in the nomination of the Commission have already been mentioned in the previous subchapter. Let us now return to our main topic and study the correspondence of the core governmental functions between and among EU institutions as well as between the two levels of European governance from the angle of the EP.

In the European Parliament, the Parliamentary Committees represent the sectoral structure subdividing the overall tasks of that institution. In a general approach, the 20 core governmental functions we have identified in the beginning are well covered by 19 EP committees. (See Table 4) However, the distribution of the sectors shows a rather uneven picture. Ten parliamentary committees center around five important governmental functions (internal affairs, justice, foreign affairs, monetary policy and agriculture) following a mostly sensible task division. At the same time, four committees (IMCO, ITRE, ENVI, TRAN)[11] are multifunctional and cover altogether nine governmental functions. Table 4 helps to state that in some committees of this second category the combination of the areas covered is not necessarily realistic. For example, while the EP Committees dealing with the internal market as well as with questions related to industry are logical combinations of different sectors, better matches could have been found for certain components of environment and transport as part of other committees.

Table 4. National governmental functions and the European Parliament

Governmental Functions	EP Committees	
	Name	
Internal affairs	Civil Liberties, Justice and Home Affairs	*LIBE*
Justice	Legal Affairs	*JURI*
Foreign affairs	Foreign Affairs	*AFET*
	Human Rights	*DROI*
	Security and Defense	*SEDE*
External trade	International Trade	*INTA*
Development cooperation	Development	*DEVE*
Financial and monetary policy	Economic and Monetary Affairs	*ECO*
	Budgets	*BUDG*
	Budgetary Control	*CONT*
Economic, social and territorial cohesion	Regional Development	*REGI*
Internal market	Internal Market and Consumer Protection	*IMCO*
Consumer protection		
Competition policy	---	

---

11 Respectively Internal Market and Consumer Protection; Industry, Research and Energy; Environment, Public Health and Food Safety; Transport and Tourism. See the abbreviated names of the EP Committees in Table 4.

Industry	Industry, Research and Energy	ITRE
Research and development		
Energy		
Agriculture and fisheries	Agriculture and Rural Development	AGRI
	Fisheries	PECH
Environment	Environment, Public Health and Food Safety	ENVI
Public health		
Transport, telecommunication	Transport and Tourism	TRAN
Tourism		
Education and vocational training	Culture and Education	CULT
Social policy	Employment and Social Affairs	EMPL

Source: Own compilation.

All in all, however, the sectoral subdivision of the EP Committees' tasks comes the closest to the pragmatic governmental needs considering the governance structures of both member states and the European Union. Therefore, the vertical correspondence of the governmental functions and the Parliamentary Committees is quite accurate. Still, if we were to compare the parliamentary committees of the European Parliament and those of the national parliaments, we would in all likelihood find that it differs from country to country.

Vertical and horizontal coherence in the system as a whole

After having paid due attention to the vertical axis of sectoral connections of European governance, let us now proceed to a parallel comparison of the sectoral structures of the three main EU institutions and the list of core governmental functions we identified on the national level. (See Table 5) This comparison will enable us to draw conclusions concerning the quality of overall horizontal coherence in the EU in its sectoral aspects.

Table 5. National governmental functions and the European institution

Governmental Functions	Council of the European Union	European Commission	EP Committees
Internal affairs	Justice and Home Affairs Council	Home affairs *(Cecilia Malmström)*	Legal Affairs *(JURI)*
Justice		Justice, fundamental rights and citizenship *(Viviane Reding)*	Civil Liberties, Justice and Home Affairs *(LIBE)*

Foreign affairs	Foreign Affairs Council	High Representative of the Union for foreign affairs and security policy *(Catherine Ashton)* Enlargement and neighborhood policy *(Stefan Füle)*	Foreign Affairs *(AFET)* Human Rights *(DROI)* Security and Defense *(SEDE)*
External trade		Trade *(Karel De Gucht)*	International Trade *(INTA)*
Development cooperation		Development *(Andris Piebalgs)* International cooperation, humanitarian aid and crisis response *(Kristalina Georgieva)*	Development *(DEVE)*
Agriculture and fisheries	Agriculture and Fisheries Council	Agriculture and rural development *(Dacian Ciolos)* Maritime affairs and fisheries *(Maria Damanaki)*	Agriculture and Rural Development *(AGRI)* Fisheries *(PECH)*
Financial and monetary policy	Economic and Financial Affairs Council	Economic and monetary affairs *(Olli Rehn)* Financial programming and budget *(Janusz Lewandowski)* Taxation and customs union, audit and anti-fraud *(Algirdas Semeta)*	Economic and Monetary Affairs (ECON) Budgets (BUDG) Budgetary Control (CONT)
Economic, social and territorial cohesion		Regional policy *(Johannes Hahn)*	Regional Development (REGI)
Competition policy		Competition *(Joaquín Almunia)*	---
Environment	Environment Council	Climate action *(Connie Hedegaard)* Environment *(Janez Potocnik)*	Environment, Public Health and Food Safety (ENVI)
Public health	Employment, Social Policy, Health and Consumer Affairs Council	Health *(Tonio Borg)*	
Social policy		Employment, social affairs and inclusion *(László Andor)*	Employment and Social Affairs (EMPL)
Consumer protection		Consumer protection *(Neven Mimica)*	Internal Market and Consumer Protection (IMCO)

Internal market	Competitiveness Council	Internal market and services *(Michel Barnier)*	
Industry		Industry and entrepreneurship *(Antonio Tajani)*	Industry, Research and Energy (ITRE)
Research and development		Research, innovation and science *(Méire Geoghegann-Quinn)*	
Energy	Transport, elecommunications and Energy Council	Energy *(Günther Oettinger)*	
Transport, tele-communication		Transport *(Siim Kallas)* Digital agenda *(Neelie Kroes)*	Transport and Tourism (TRAN)
Tourism	---	---	
Education and vocational training	Education, Youth, Culture and Sport	Education, culture, multilingualism, youth *(Androulla Vassiliou)*	Culture and Education (CULT)

Source: Own compilation.

Concerning the horizontal coherence of the sectors on the community level, the picture is rather complex. We barely see any clear sectoral profiles connecting the top EU institutions with each other, while overlaps among institutional configurations (Council formations, EP committees etc.) with various profiles are relatively common. The strongest horizontal coherence is visible in the field of agriculture and fisheries, which is one of the most traditional policy areas of European integration, as well as in the field of education, which is a sector under the supporting competence of the EU only. In both cases we see one council formation, one Commissioner's portfolio and one parliamentary committee dealing with the given sector. Bearing in mind that the number of EU Council formations is artificially low and that, for this reason, most of them include several sectors, the next level of comparison is between the Commission portfolios and the parliamentary committees. Here we can find almost perfect coherence when the Commission portfolios and the parliamentary committees are well aligned with each other and both fall under the same council formation. This is the case e.g. with external trade, development cooperation, regional cohesion or social policy (employment and social affairs).

Again due to the low number of council configurations and their concise profiles, it might be worth considering not only individual governmental functions but also "blocks" of governmental functions and to investigate whether they appear coherently on the EU institutional level. On this issue we consider a block to be coherent if all Commission portfolios and all parliamentary committees dealing with the sectors in question fall under the same council configuration. Here, we can see a relatively high level of horizontal coherence in important sectors:

- *Justice and internal affairs:* one council, two EP committees, two Commissioners;
- *Foreign affairs, including development and external trade:* one council, five EP committees, five Commissioners;

- *Financial and monetary policy, economic, social and territorial cohesion and competition policy:* one council, four EP committees, five Commissioners.

  However, there is a striking difference between the extremely concentrated profile of the Council formations and the high number of both EP committees and Commissioners dealing with the same sectoral area. A real shortcoming here is the lack of a parliamentary committee responsible for competition policy; there is no official body in the European Parliament that would represent the interests of EU citizens in the field of competition.

  It should be seen that the strong horizontal "block" coherence is typical of sectors that have been traditionally areas of common governance and where EU institutions exercise strong power themselves. As we move towards sectors which are under supporting EU competence, we see the horizontal coherence weakening and becoming dislocated. Examples are:

- *Environment and public health:* two councils, one EP committee, three Commissioners. The profile of the environment sector would be almost completely clear if its parliamentary committee did not also deal with public health. While one can to some extent argue for a combination of the two topics, the problem is that environment has its own council formation, while public health is discussed at the Employment, Social Policy, Health and Consumer Affairs Council.

- *Consumer protection and internal market:* two councils, one EP committee, two Commissioners. Although individual Commissioners deal with the two sectors insofar as they are covered by the same parliamentary committee (where the sectoral combination is absolutely reasonable), they belong to two different and very complex council configurations, which never meet with one another: consumer protection is under the Employment, Social Policy, Health and Consumer Affairs Council dealing with social issues, while internal market belongs to the Competitiveness Council working mostly on economic development questions.

- *Industry, research and energy:* two councils, one EP committee, three Commissioners. The three sectors are covered by the same parliamentary committee, which is a sensible combination, but the depth of EU competences is strikingly different: in industry and research the EU only has "supporting" competence; while in the field of energy it has shared competence with the member states. Moreover, industry and research are discussed in the Competitiveness Council, while energy is under the supervision of the Transport, Telecommunications and Energy Council.

- *Transport, telecommunication and tourism:* one council, one EP committee, two Commissioners. Interestingly, transport was one of the first sectors in which common governance was introduced already in the Treaty of Rome, yet the sector's horizontal coherence is still weak institutionally. Considering the number of institutions responsible for the three interrelated sectors, the overall coherence seems strong, but the main problem is the lack of fora in the Council and the Commission discussing the important sector of tourism. This means that no formation represents expressly the interests of the member states and of the EU on that matter, while a specific parliamentary committee deals with it. In institutional terms, tourism seems to be the most underrepresented governmental function in the main EU institutions.

Conclusions

In this chapter, we sought to examine the institutional frameworks for cooperation and co-ordination in areas of common sectoral governance in the European Union. We have examined also the depth of horizontal and vertical coherence within the EU and between the Union and its member states, which we consider to be an indicator of the quality of sectoral governance. We are deeply convinced that strong vertical and horizontal ties are prerequisites of good EU governance.

We found that due to the highly concentrated policy functions of the different configurations of the EU Council, vertical and horizontal coherence are the least strong here. At the other end of the spectrum, we found that the European Commission with 26 Commissioners (without its President and one of the vice-presidents) covered all but one key governmental functions. In some cases, even more than one Commissioner is working on various individual aspects of the same sectoral policy area. The division of sectoral policies into smaller sub-sectoral areas, however, overstates the individual importance of some of the smaller portfolios. Based on our comparisons, we found that the internal structure of the European Parliament with its 19 specific sectoral committees comes closest to the ideal division of government tasks we set up as a model, and opens the way to the strongest vertical and horizontal coherence among the EU institutions as well as between the EU and its member states.

With regards to the horizontal coherence of sectoral governance in the three main EU institutions, we have found a mixed picture. Only two areas (agriculture – including fisheries – and education) possess clear and coherent inter-institutional profiles, one of which (CAP) is a traditional sector of common governance. Certain "blocks" (strongly connected sectoral areas) of governmental functions also have coherent inter-institutional coverage. This is first and foremost true of important, wider governmental functions, where the EU has either exclusive or shared competences, and thus a longer history of common governance. The area of justice and home affairs as well as foreign affairs (including external trade and development cooperation), or the wide scope of the economic and monetary sector belong here. Nonetheless, governmental functions, which are under shared competence and have been covered by the EU only more recently, or where additional small functions entered the picture with the "big bang" enlargement of 2004, do not have a coherent profile. This is especially worrisome in the case of sectors considered under the Competitiveness Council (internal market, industry, research and development) given that the EU is still aiming to increase its competitiveness in the world.

All in all, our analysis showed that there are serious shortcomings with regards to both the vertical and horizontal coherence of European sectoral governance. In certain cases, such shortcomings even result in the lack of representation of member states' and citizens' interest at the European level. Such situations can also question the legitimacy of EU decisions in some areas. An equally worrisome result of our analysis is the complexity of coordination, and hence the low efficiency of European governance. In order to overcome the current economic and political challenges (of growth and jobs, world-wide competitiveness, stability of the Eurozone as well as further enlargement), the EU would need to undergo certain institutional reforms. Such reforms should target, among others, the strengthening of horizontal coherence of European governance by aligning the various council formations and EP committees with each other to avoid situations where a parliamentary committee has to coordinate its policy making with two council formations. However, to help strengthen the vertical sectoral coherence of governance between the EU operational level and national government institutions, reforms at the EU level are not sufficient: it would be necessary for the member states to become more open to aligning their sectoral governmental structures for the benefit of common EU governance.

Bibliography

Balázs, P. (2014a). Enlargement Conditionality of the European Union and Future Prospects. In I. Govaere, E. Lannon, P. Van Elsuwege & S. Adam, *The European Union in the World. Essays in Honour of Marc Maresceau* (pp. 523-540). Leiden – Boston: Martinus Nijhoff Publishers.

Balázs, P. (2014b). EU 36. The impact of EU enlargement on institutions. In P. Balázs, *A European Union with 36 members? Perspectives and risks* (pp. 227-255). Budapest: CEU Press.

Benz, A. & Zimmer C. (2010). The EU's competences: The 'vertical' perspective on the multilevel system. *Living Reviews in European Governance*. 5(1), 1-31.

Haas, E. B. (1958). *The uniting of Europe: Political, social, and economic forces 1950-57*. Stanford, CA: Stanford University Press.

Pollack, M. A. (2000). The end of creeping competence? EU policy-making since Maastricht. *Journal of Common Market Studies*. 38(3), 519-538.

Schmitter, P. (1969). Three neofunctional hypotheses about international integration. *International Organization*. 23(1), 161-166.

Schmitter, P. C. (1996). Imagining the future of the Euro-polity with the help of new concepts. In G. Marks, F.G. Scharpf, P.C. Schmitter & W. Streeck, *Governance in the European Union* (pp. 121-165). London: Sage.

Vesnic-Alujevic, L. & Nacarino, R. C. (2012). The EU and its democratic deficit: problems and (possible) solutions. *European View*. June 2013, 63-70.

A CRISIS IN NEVERLAND: THE FUTURE OF EU FOREIGN POLICY AND THE ROLE OF LARGE MEMBER STATES

ANDRÁS SZALAI

The year 2014 marks a number of anniversaries in Europe. A hundred years ago, the continent was engulfed in the flames of the First World War; twenty-five years ago, Europe was once again united after forty years of Cold War brinksmanship; and ten years ago, the European Union (EU) took an enormous step towards further unifying the old continent as eight post-communist states joined the Union as members. For these symbolic historical anniversaries alone, 2014 should be a year of self-reflection in Europe. But other, current events also call for reconsidering the past and, pragmatically, looking to the future. The ongoing financial crisis, shifting global power relations, a cooling transatlantic bond, and a Russia questioning the post-Cold War *status quo* all challenge the EU as a polity, and will force it to adjust its policy tools, both internal and external. Yet the EU in 2014 looks more fragmented, more inward-looking and contentious than ever before. The financial crisis especially is testing the social, political and economic fabric of the Union, threatening to stall or even reverse the integration process. Yet, despite growing levels of Euroscepticism among its citizens, Europe needs to be the solution, not the problem: the pan-European debate needs to continue among member states, both among their elites and their citizenry.

However, focusing on internal issues must not mean a parallel neglect of the EU's role as a global player, since foreign and enlargement policy will remain key policy tools with potential positive domestic effects. Conversely, isolation would decrease the EU's impact on world affairs, which in turn may hinder growth in the Union. Non-action can take its toll in many ways, as we are witnessing in the case of the ongoing crisis in East Ukraine. Coordinating these often seemingly contradictory goals requires leadership from within the EU – something the organization is severely lacking at the moment. In the absence of the Monnets and Delors of our age, member states as actors must take leadership.

In line with this assumption, this chapter aims to do two things. First, it discusses the nature and implications of a foreign policy identity crisis in the European Union. Reviewing the institutional and political manifestations of the EU as an international actor, as well as its track record, the chapter establishes that the EU suffers from two interrelated problems. On the one hand, it is leaderless, meaning its potential for foreign policy identity-building measures amidst the current political turmoil is questionable. On the other hand, member states are acutely aware of the Union's ongoing political crisis and are becoming more inward-looking: they revert to intergovernmental practices in a process called "the silent revolution." (Buras, 2013) This trend, I will argue, is likely to impact on EU foreign policy as foreign policy is still a symbolic element of state sovereignty: member states skeptical of the EU are more likely to rely on "renationalized" foreign policy positions and moves.[1]

The second goal of the chapter is to offer an analytical toolkit to assess this fluid situation in terms of its effects on EU actorness and the corresponding foreign policy identity. The current foreign policy identity crisis, coupled with the reversal towards intergovernmentalism, creates a threat that states will rely on narrow, national foreign policies which in turn would make a truly European foreign policy meaningless, even unfeasible. This, however, does not necessarily mean a reversal to narrow-minded geopolitics. With the European-level identity in crisis, the position of important, large states' position on matters of EU foreign policy will be of crucial importance. Therefore, the second half of the chapter reviews existing foreign policy analysis (FPA) approaches that could be applied – either separately or through a synthesis – to specifically targeted large member states in a European context. This second element, building on the path-breaking work of Erik Larsen (2009), is offered so that analysts can better assess both the existing foreign policy traditions of these states, and the interaction between the current political environment and these traditions.

The underlying assumption the chapter builds on is that the identity crisis resulting from the EU's problems necessitates identity-building on the state level. Big states carry special importance in this respect and, based on the dominant theoretical literature, pre-existing foreign policy identities in these states will set the future course of a European foreign policy identity. But this is by no means a deterministic process: geopolitical Europe looms in the background, not necessarily in terms of a return to the 19th century, but in the sense of the EU becoming an empty rhetorical device in foreign policy terms used by national states to reinforce their standing globally, and even to gather eurosceptic support domestically.

European foreign policy: from euphoria to crisis

The intensity of cooperation on matters of foreign policy within the European Union has been steadily increasing in the past 30-odd years: giving a voice to the EU as a global player has been a central concern of member states ever since the creation of the European Political Cooperation (EPC) in 1970. A common foreign policy has repeatedly been justified as the next logical step in integration, in continuing the European project, and imbuing the EU with its own identity in world politics. This quest for European presence and visibility in the international arena has been supported by the creation of the Common Foreign and Security Policy (CFSP) pillar in the 1990s, as well as by the founding of the European External Action Service (EEAS) in 2010. The gradual institutionalization of the policy field shows commitment to the idea of a *European* foreign policy and is supposed to signal that it is not an ephemeral phenomenon.

Academic research offers useful ways of understanding these policies from a conceptual

---

1   European foreign policy is a structured coordination process among a very diverse group of member states. The central element, the Common Foreign and Security Policy, is decidedly intergovernmental, yet some external actions, most notably enlargement, already involve the Commission and the "Community method." Nevertheless, in practice, national foreign policies often prevail over a common approach. Thus, without actual EU competences in the field, a renationalization seems more straightforward than in other policy areas.

point of view. By the mid-2000s, European Studies as a discipline had witnessed exponential growth in the literature on Europe (a term used interchangeably with the EU) as a global player. Reflecting the general optimism among Brussels' and member states' elites about the future of the European project, scholars emphasized the *sui generis* nature of the EU as a foreign policy actor, arguing that the EU wields power that is different from power tradition-ally understood, but is equally effective. The argument went that the Union primarily relies on means that fall under the category of "soft power" (Nye, 2004, 2011), instead of hard – primarily military – power, in order to achieve its foreign policy objectives. In doing so, the EU acts as a normative, magnetic anchor for other states, thereby stabilizing its immediate neighborhood and defining what counts as normal in international relations. This rather passive role interpretation was to be coupled with more active foreign policy instruments, including the creation of a European diplomatic corps with delegations worldwide, as well as a more active military presence that nevertheless retains its emphasis on "civilian ele-ments." (Jørgensen, 2004)

However, how this conceptual framework relates to practice is a source of contention. Turning the idea of a common foreign and security policy into practice came with a number of ethical challenges, as well as a mixed record. In practice, despite an increasing number of foreign missions, the EU's performance in creating a coherent common policy position in various crisis situations, or *vis-à-vis* global competitors such as China, has been uneven at best. Often at the epicenter of the issue is the lack of common positions, which highlights an important problem with European foreign policy: it is still not *European*. In 2014, despite the increasing role of Brussels-based institutions – particularly that of the EEAS – foreign policy still remains an intergovernmental policy field. Nation states find it hard to relinquish their sovereignty in matters of foreign affairs, and their diverging interests mean a common European position on pivotal problems such as the Middle East occurs all too infrequently. This fragmentation can in part explain the gap between expectations and reality in terms of CFSP performance. Consequently, from the analyst's point of view, member states matter more than the EU when it comes to European foreign policy, and they matter very visibly, especially larger member states with a capable, proactive foreign policy tradition.

Lack of an EU foreign policy is, however, only part of the problem: today's Europe is leaderless and is in a state of policy flux. No member state is willing to openly bear the burden of offering a clear vision for the European project, and, without a clear end point, political insecurities in the wake of the current political and economic crisis negatively affect the continued development of the EU's common foreign policy. The general euphoria of the early 2000s about an EU that is able to act as a unified international *actor* is all but gone, and Europe is left with the negative feedback loop described above.

Javier Solana once described it as a global superpower (Solana, 2005), yet when it comes to its foreign policy the EU still faces a capability-expectations gap, lacks the institutional channels necessary for effective foreign policy aggregation, possesses fragmented policy goals (take for instance the awkward regional focus of the European Neighbourhood Policy) and its relation with major partners is still characterized by bilateralism. (Wong, 2010) But can a truly European foreign policy, a "Neverland" – something that never was – be in crisis? As this analysis maintains, the crisis in question is not necessarily about foreign policy instru-ments, but about the underlying vision that defines Europe's foreign policy identity. The capability-expectations gap between global actorness and the developments – or lack there-of – of the past decade has left the EU, as well as its member states that relied on the Union as part of their identity, with a foreign policy identity crisis. Not having fulfilled the requirements contained within its previous conception of its role as a global actor, and lacking a truly defining leader, the EU needs to escape from this "identity limbo" and to construct a new identity in order to represent its interests more effectively.

What this identity will look like is a fundamental question for the coming years, and it brings us back to elementary questions of political integration: will the new identity/identities be conceived of at the supranational or at the national level? Will a new, *common* conception of identity emerge, or rather a loose collection of national foreign policies that might even weaken any attempt at forming a common position?

Politics and policies: foreign affairs on two levels

The difference and frequent opposition between perceived domestic and European interests has gained in strength throughout the current multi-faceted and multi-layered crisis. Shifts in global power, the Eurozone crisis, the resulting political turmoil, the apparent overstretch resulting from enlargement, and the rise of regional rivals, all push European states towards being more inward-looking. Coupled with the oft-mentioned democracy deficit of the EU, i.e. the detachment of the unaccountable technocratic elite in Brussels from the average European citizen, these changes heighten the importance of domestic politics. (See Zürn & de Wilde, 2012) Certain shifts towards nationalism in voting patterns all over Europe – especially in those member states that are most affected by the economic crisis – further undermine business-as-usual policy making on the supranational level. (See e.g. Fligstein, Polyakova, & Sandholtz, 2012) Such problems are met with a lack of both political leadership and vision, which leads to a foreign policy identity crisis and a return to intergovernmentalism in European politics.

This identity crisis has two separate levels. On the one hand it is a crisis of the CFSP, and involves the negative identity of the EU as a non-actor. On the other hand it is a crisis of the Europeanized foreign policies of member states that seem to be losing the supranational umbrella that has supported them in foreign policy terms. For them, a new identity needs to be created that takes into account the failure/limits of the CFSP. This latter type of identity crisis is especially acute for states that have given a central position to the EU within their foreign policy identity: Germany, for instance, does not for historical reasons have a non-EU related foreign policy identity it can easily fall back onto.

In order to highlight the potential tension between the two levels, the chapter departs from the popular distinction made in this section's title: the perceived opposition between politics and policies. Politics is often used with negative connotations: it is considered cynical, interest-based, petty, corrupt and ineffective. Policy on the other hand is frequently seen as removed from the chaotic realm of politics – i.e. from what politicians do – and is imbued with an aura of rational expertise. Thus policy is what experts (not bureaucrats!) do, and its goal is to maximize the public interest. This over-exaggerated popular distinction is, as the extensive literature on bureaucratic politics shows (Allison, 1972; Drezner, 2000; Weldes, 1998), quite untenable, yet it is a useful point of departure for discussing dynamics between national politics and EU-level technocratic policy making. Nowhere is this opposition more apparent than in the field of foreign policy, where state governments still hold their ground.

Within the field of European Studies, this duality between the two levels is assessed through the concept of Europeanization. Following Radaelli, I understand Europeanization as a concept that refers to:

> processes of (a) construction (b) diffusion and (c) institutionalisation of formal and informal rules, procedures, policy paradigms, styles, 'ways of doing things' and shared beliefs and norms which are first defined and consolidated in the making of EU decisions and then incorporated in the logic of domestic discourse, identities, political structures and public policies. (Radaelli, 2003, p. 30)

In this dominant interpretation, Europeanization therefore explains how the process of integration has a top-down effect on domestic politics and policies.

From the member state perspective, the dominant strand of literature within European Studies, liberal institutionalism, explains foreign policy integration through state interests: member states seek to promote a common foreign policy because it lends them greater global visibility and influence than their own resources and subject position would merit. (Moravcsik, 2010) Yet integration in this particular field is obviously incomplete: Brussels does not have absolute decision-making authority. Therefore, member states have a number of possibilities for pursuing their foreign policy goals: they can act through the EU; through another international institution such as the North Atlantic Treaty Organization (NATO); they can rely on bilateralism in their relations; or make unilateral moves. Thus far it has been generally assumed that whenever a member state acts through the EU, it can thereby reinforce its own position – this has been the instrumental logic behind a common foreign policy from the beginning. With integration still in a transitional state, the central question for the academic literature is how much space member states are willing to cede to the Union in terms of foreign policy. How individual states assess the question will have a fundamental impact on the evolution of the EU's role-conception in world politics.

Because it works in both directions, Europeanization acts as a link between the two levels: state interests influence and shape common policies on the European level, while European policies and institutions socialize member state decision-makers and enable/constrain national policies. Thus the current state of flux in terms of the future of the CFSP and the role conception of the Union embedded within it are not necessarily about instrumentally using Europe to further national agendas in foreign policy but, on the contrary, about the extent to which nation states have adopted European preferences in foreign policy matters and the extent to which they believe the EU is capable of acting on these preferences as an organization. (Gross, 2011, p. xiii)

When it comes to visions of Europe's role in the world, and given the lack of proper institutionalization in foreign policy matters – the EEAS still being in its infancy – the vision(s) of large member states appear pivotal. Frequently only large states have the resources and indeed the necessary foreign policy culture to form preferences with reference to a global role. Lower level policy making, on the other hand, is relegated to technocrats in EU institutions. Their size and influence within the EU singles out these states, but it is also important to note that they often have diverging views on European affairs, broadly understood. For instance, when it comes to the European Security and Defence Policy (ESDP), Gross (2011) identifies Britain as the Atlanticist, France as the Europeanist and Germany as the in-between power with often contradictory positions on key foreign policy matters.

Dreams of global normative power

Initially an economic project, the idea of a common foreign policy identity tied to the EU's global responsibilities as an economic power only entered the political debate in the 1990s. Two International Relations (IR) concepts are key to understanding the EU's international role: actorness (Hill, 1993; Jupille & Caporaso, 1998) and presence (Allen & Smith, 1990; Elgström & Smith, 2006). Actorness defines the characteristics and prerequisites of being an international actor: 1) recognition by outsiders, 2) authority, i.e. the legal competence to act, 3) autonomy (distinctiveness and independence from other international actors) and 4) cohesion (the extent to which it is seen as a unitary actor from outside). (Jupille & Caporaso, 1998) The EU still falls short of these requirements. All it has been able to achieve is a global presence whereby it shapes and filters the perceptions of other policy-makers especially in the economic sphere. (Allen & Smith, 1990) This ability to shape what counts as normal in international affairs through civilian means later became the core of the EU's self-image, captured under the concept of "normative power Europe," a concept that married the academic and the policy discourse. (Manners, 2008)

According to the concept of normative power, the EU "acts by being:" maintaining a common European identity and projecting it outwards as a form of magnetic pull is in itself a foreign policy act, especially visible in its immediate neighborhood that we now commonly refer to as "wider Europe."[2] (Lucarelli & Manners, 2006) The EU continues to defy Westphalian notions of international actorness: it is of course not a state, and relies more on civilian instruments than on military power. Its complex creation, evolution and structure continue to puzzle academics. In Andrew Moravcsik's words, "in few areas of interstate politics are ideas so often invoked, identities so clearly at stake, and interests so complex, challenging and uncertain." (Moravcsik, 1999, p. 669)

Another part of the European Union's uniqueness as a political entity stems from its policy-making structure: the practice of pooling the sovereignty of its member states. Since the Treaty of Rome (1957), various competencies that were previously the exclusive prerogatives of sovereign states have been delegated to the supranational level. But foreign policy, a key defining element of a sovereign state, has been lagging behind, posing a difficult question to proponents of European actorness: without its own foreign policy, how can the Union be an actor? Instead, we see diverging member state interests on matters of foreign policy, and an inconsistent, weak policy instrument on the European level.

"Normative power Europe" offers a conceptual solution to this problem by stating that the EU now *is* and *acts as* an embodiment of norms, and that as such it possesses a much larger influence in world politics than capabilities-based approaches, which in this case would focus on the EU's economic might, would suggest. The theory proposes that certain characteristics of the EU's organization predispose it to act in a normative way: universal norms and principles are at the center of the EU's relations with member states and other actors in world politics, so the Union's foreign relations are more informed by a "catalogue of norms" than is the case with other international actors. Ian Manners, the originator of the concept, also

---

2   Moreover, some argue that the relationship is in fact reflexive: an assertive foreign policy can be used to further integration. From this angle, foreign policy has to be seen as the next logical phase of integration. (See Bickerton, 2013)

argues that these norms and principles are the basis of a distinct European identity.[3] He argues that "the central component of normative power Europe is that it exists as being different to pre-existing political forms, and this particular difference pre-disposes it to act in a normative way." (Manners, 2002, p. 242) As such, the EU *acts by being*, and seeks to shape the international system via its passive image. For proponents of "normative power Europe," the EU acts as a normative beacon, a prosperous paradise that compels other nations to assume European norms – norms through which the EU has redefined what counts as "normal" in world politics. Importantly, this power is only sustainable if it is felt to be legitimate by those who practice and experience it. (Manners & Whitman, 2003; Manners, 2002, 2006, 2008)

Theoretically, this understanding of actorness does not require a *bona fide* foreign policy. However, as recent trends have highlighted, magnetism has very serious limits. The failure of the EU's Eastern Partnership in particular shows that soft power needs to be backed by hard power, but also that a unified European position is necessary for the EU to appear credible towards both its neighbors and its rivals. Though the EU was largely successful in reshaping its immediate environment after the end of the Cold War, a more active foreign policy would now be needed to maintain a global presence, not to mention a "superpower" role. Yet despite these issues, the concept of normative power enjoys popularity to this day both in academic and in EU policy circles, showing the influence of academic theorizing on policy making, if only in rhetorical terms. The slow initial pace of the CFSP/ESDP process – especially in the military domain – and the EU's failed stabilization attempts in the Balkans had reinforced the conviction shared by many analysts that Europe's strength does and should lie in its civilian instruments and normative attainments. (Rosencrance, 1998, p. 22) How policy instruments were created to channel the EU's normative identity into foreign policy terms is the topic of the next section.

The External Action Service: the EU's means to global presence?

A Secure Europe, the security strategy of the European Union, was created at the turn of the millennium and reflected the general optimism surrounding the EU's global aspirations. (*European Security Strategy: A Secure Europe in a Better World*, 2003) Through it the Union repositioned itself as a global, rather than a regional, actor, with a range of military and civilian instruments. This new role has been articulated in the discourse of universal ethics that defines the EU as a "peacebuilder" or "a force of good," thereby legitimizing the Union's role in global politics. (Aggestam, 2008) Crucially, *A Secure Europe* also enabled the acquisition of military capabilities,[4] and since 2002, the EU has intervened militarily on 19 different occasions.

---

3   The existence of a common European identity based on a common history and culture is a constant source of debate. Hill, for example, would disagree with Manners' argument by maintaining that "the EU rests on a relatively weak sense of shared history and identity because of the diverse historical experiences of its members, the EU's lack of influence over education, and its inability to create and manipulate stated goals which national governments themselves use to strengthen communal identities." (Quoted in Ginsberg, 1999, p. 436) Nevertheless, even Hill acknowledges that the EU is increasingly associated with a distinct set of principles.

4   Larsen (2002) also identifies a competing discourse on the EU acquiring military capabilities.

Yet despite its growing number of missions abroad, the European Union still struggles to translate its economic and political might into a comparable level of influence. Some of the arguments that might explain this discrepancy have already been mentioned, most importantly the EU's structure of sovereign members states with diverse agendas, and the lack of shared or exclusive external competences in the foreign policy field. These problems are of course well-known among European and national elites, and have been the subject of the reform process that culminated in the Lisbon Treaty (in force since late 2009). The most crucial aspect of the Treaty for this chapter is the creation of the External Action Service – the quasi-autonomous institutional manifestation of European civilian power – and a corresponding high level position within the Council: the High Representative of the Union for Foreign Affairs and Security Policy (HR/VP), first occupied by Catherine Ashton. The treaty of Lisbon defines the role of the HR in the following terms:

> The High Representative shall represent the Union for matters relating to the common foreign and security policy. He shall conduct political dialogue with third parties on the Union's behalf and shall express the Union's position in international organisations and at international conferences. (Article 27(2) TEU)

Apart from his/her task as the head of EU diplomacy, the HR also acts as the Vice President of the European Commission.

The creation of a common diplomatic corps and a single position to represent the EU abroad was to lend the necessary institutional background to building up the EU's image as a unified, stand-alone diplomatic actor worldwide. Still, decision-making authority was only partially transferred from nation states, so that the EU's intergovernmental origins remain intact. This development is an organic extension of the Europeanization process: by institutionalizing the oft-referenced pooling of sovereignty in the foreign policy field within the EU bureaucracy, the EEAS is "Europeanizing" national foreign policy. (Wong & Hill, 2011) Yet the EEAS has not changed the rules of the game in the past three years. Could the problem be one of translating member state interests into a coherent position? Or does the political and institutional flux of the crisis hinder further integration in the foreign policy field?

Critics of the EEAS see its policy of operation – Ashton's "quiet diplomacy" – as one of its fundamental problems. As mentioned earlier, the gap between a foreign policy identity constructed in the political discourse, and actual, on the ground performance has been a continuous challenge for the CSFP in the 21st century, the discrepancy keeping the EU from achieving the global presence it seeks. Therefore quiet diplomacy, a term lifted from the pages of the Cold War and that argued for careful behind the scenes maneuvering with a focus on conflict prevention and compromise, may not be the best guiding principle for a new organization for a crisis-ridden EU that seeks greater influence and presence on the global stage. More a buzzword than substantive policy, quiet diplomacy lacks real content, and could sometimes be confused with plain silence even on key issues. (Lyon, 2010) In addition, quiet diplomacy is only able to promise a limited scope of action when both the EU's ambitions and the range of issues it is invested in globally are expanding. Humanitarian catastrophes such as the earthquake in Haiti, military conflicts such as the civil war in Syria, or the negotiations on the EU-US Free Trade Agreement, offer very diverse challenges that cannot always be addressed through backdoor diplomacy, leaving the EEAS and its leader open to both internal and global criticism.

But the policy of its current leader is not the EEAS' only problem. Even though the Service has quasi-autonomy, it is far from being the only forum for EU foreign policy decision making. Finding a strong, common position is rendered hard by differences among member states, or even between the Council and the Commission. This convoluted network of interests limits the HR to basic statements of little substance. Consequently, given the lack of visibility of the office *designed* to represent a European position globally, one again returns to the problem of intergovernmentalism, i.e. the vision of individual member states. Thus, the EEAS seems little more than an additional institution that extends the Brussels bureaucracy, and is unlikely to be at the forefront of a solution to the current foreign policy identity crisis. By not presenting a clear, consensual alternative, it further aggravates the problem.

The silent revolution: member states turn to intergovernmentalism

The shortcomings of the EEAS and the HR form incentives for member states to potentially return to intergovernmentalism in foreign policy making. Intergovernmentalism has a long tradition in the EU's history as powerful European states have often engaged in traditional concert diplomacy to circumvent, or empower, the CFSP/ESDP. The Big Three platform in the negotiations on Iran's nuclear program, or the 2011 multi-state intervention in Libya, are examples of this. While the normative rhetoric is often there,[5] and the EU may also be present as a separate entity, such cases show the limits of a common European foreign policy, limits which debilitate the quasi-actorness of the European Union. Realist scholars have long argued that the EU should be seen merely as an intervening variable when it comes to transmitting large state interest to the global level (see e.g. Hyde-Price, 2006), but the current return to state-level foreign policy represents a qualitative change that goes beyond the realist argument and therefore requires closer scrutiny.

In a recent article for the European Council on Foreign Relations (ECFR), Buras (2013) argues that the economic crisis and the resulting political-institutional crisis in the EU have led to a "silent revolution" where "the supranational dream of European federation is giving way to an intergovernmental approach, a default mechanism necessitated by the impossibility of treaty change and the interests of major EU members."[6] This revolution currently affects the economic sphere, Buras explains, but it will also likely affect other policy fields in the future. Though a return to intergovernmentalism might solve some of the gridlock inherent in EU decision making, it is also likely to exacerbate other problems. It is not difficult to imagine that the "revolution" will reach foreign policy, and potentially exclude pro-integration elites from the renegotiation of the EU's foreign policy identity. Already the foreign policy gap between Brussels and national capitals has hindered a unified approach on several occasions, most notably with regards to EU-China relations, as the ECFR scorecard attests year after year.[7] The ongoing economic and political crisis in the Eurozone further

---

5   Neorealism, a fundamentally behavioralist theory, disregards state rhetoric and focuses exclusively on state action that in turn can be explained by structural factors, such as anarchy and the current distribution of power.

6   The ECFR scorecard from 2013 seems to support this claim. See http://www.ecfr.eu/scorecard/2013.

7   The ECFR Scorecard offers a systematic annual assessment of the EU's performance in dealing with the rest of the world. The expert/stakeholder survey is coordinated by the think tank, and is conducted by

widens this gap: crisis-stricken countries such as Spain have been forced to target their limited resources on areas of specific national interest, rather than on wider aims that fall under the purview of the EU's global role.

The Big Three are of crucial importance in such a fluid situation. The United Kingdom can still be considered as committed to Europe on foreign policy matters, and a driver of European foreign policy despite its Prime Minister David Cameron's eurosceptic views and the rise of its anti-European party UK Independence Party (UKIP).[8] The Franco-German engine of Europe, on the other hand, seems to be less visible in foreign policy matters, as for example Germany's conciliatory, even passive approach to the Ukrainian crisis, seems to indicate. Practice shows that the EU often relies on broad coalitions of diverse member states when taking a common position, and such coalitions seldom involve both these states. Even outside the EU, Franco-German coalitions are often absent, as exemplified by German opposition to, and French-British support for, both the 2011 multinational military mission in Libya and a potential US military strike against the Syrian regime during the summer of 2013.[9] Unilateral action by European member states in the case of the UN-mandated intervention in Libya, and the complete failure of the stillborn EUFOR-Libya joint-EU mission in particular show the problems of common action in the security field.[10] Since member states could not agree on a joint CSDP operation, EUFOR-Libya was presented as a humanitarian mission, limiting its military components.

In short, a return to intergovernmentalism, or even to unilateral action, is a distinct possibility when it comes to foreign policy: as the EU is struggling with a political crisis and is unable to appear as a unified actor globally, member states that are able to do so are motivated to follow their own foreign policy agendas. What form a new type of intergovernmentalism might take, and how strong its European commitments would be, is a question for the coming decade. Nevertheless, a turn to a more state-centric self-representation does not necessarily mean Euroscepticism. Foreign policy remains a distinct policy field at the European level, and even a continued lack of a common instrument will not necessarily hinder supranational policy making in areas where EU capabilities are already strong, for example in international trade or aid policy. It also needs to be noted that rhetorically, more assertive unilateral state foreign policies might still retain a certain European orientation – as discussed previously, member states often represent individual positions as "European," and try to act as representatives of a larger body, the EU, to boost their position – and may even reignite common action. Therefore, to reiterate, leadership will be crucial for European foreign policy, which in turn will direct scholarly attention to the Big Three – the states that, due to their resources and position, are more likely to take on this role. Nevertheless, intergovernmentalism and unilateralism in the wake of the identity crisis of European foreign policy comes with its own dangers. Without a leader, coordination in a high-profile policy area such as foreign policy becomes harder and states seek new foreign policy roles that serve their perceived national interest.

---

an international team of researchers. For grades of the past four years visit http://www.ecfr.eu/score-card.

8   The 2013 ECFR scores put the UK among the leaders of EU foreign policy.

9   British support was government-only as Parliament voted down the motion.

10   The mission itself was never launched because it was made dependent on a request from the UN Office for the Co-ordination of Humanitarian Affairs (OCHA).

A negative scenario: geopolitical intergovernmentalism

The current state of the EU in general, and that of the CFSP in particular, shows a capability-expectations gap, as the ambitious goals of EU foreign policy remain unattainable and the EU does not seem to be getting closer to becoming an actor in international relations. The general shift away from community politics under the "silent revolution" will likely affect foreign policy, threatening the CFSP with becoming a very issue-specific – and consequently limited – bureaucratic affair, with the EU as a rhetorical referent for able states that follow *national* foreign policies. The current foreign policy identity crisis resulting from this widening gap and the stagnant CFSP process is reminiscent of the post-Cold War period when European states, free of the bipolar opposition, had to devise a new foreign policy identity for themselves. Let us not forget that the CFSP process itself is the result of this search for identities. However, as Guzzini's (2013) recent edited volume explains, after 1989, many European states instead returned to a particular realist position: geopolitics.

The book, *The Return to Geopolitics in Europe?,* investigates the link between international crises and foreign policy thought. The authors find that the return to geopolitics was never evident for contemporaries as many expected a wholly new era of thinking, one that does away with the political realism prevalent during the Cold War. Herein lies Guzzini et al.'s puzzle: geopolitics is a foreign policy tradition that runs counter to these expectations. As the authors argue, the revival of geopolitical thought in the 1990s can best be understood in the context of a series of foreign policy identity crises, a kind of "ontological insecurity" (Guzzini & Leander, 2006, p. 2) where previously established external norm conceptions and self-understandings are subject to change. From this change anxiety results "over a new, a newly questioned or a newly acquired self-understanding or role in world affairs," and the "spatial logic of geopolitical thought (both physical and cultural)" is then "well disposed to provide some fixtures to this anxiety." (Ibid., p. 46)

The authors identify three types of identity crises: where previous self-understandings no longer seem valid (Russia); where passive identities need to be changed to active identities (Italy); and finally where new identities need to be created or recreated (the Baltic countries or Germany). Simply put, the three archetypes mean a state of "no more identity," "no longer the previously established identity," and "no identity yet." The European Union in 2013 seems to be a strange amalgamation of these three archetypes: it did have an abstract, theorized foreign policy identity that has not materialized. So in fact the EU does not have a foreign policy identity, or at least does not have a practical one that can offer guidance in a state of political flux where the future of the European project, i.e. the possibility of federalism, is being brought into question. With a European foreign policy identity crisis, member states are stripped of the common, markedly European global role conception and are in turn thrust into their very own identity crisis: how to go on without Europe as an actor representing us all?

Mobilizing geopolitical foreign policy thought, the authors of *The Return...* find, seems to be an exceptionally well-suited tool for dealing with such an identity crisis on a national level, as it invokes material and objective guidelines for defining the national interest that can then be used to justify a wide range of policy options. Geopolitics is thus easy to communicate while also being flexible. The version of geopolitics that appeared around Europe after the fall of the Berlin wall in particular constitutes a special form of what Guzzini et al. call "neoclassical geopolitics." Neoclassical geopolitics is not just a simple return of geography to politics, but a policy-oriented analysis, generally conservative and with nationalist overtones, that gives explanatory primacy, but not exclusivity, to certain physical and human geographic factors (whether the analyst is open about this or not), and gives precedence to a strategic view, realism with a military and national gaze, for analyzing the 'objective necessities' within which states compete for power and rank. (Guzzini & Leander, 2006, p. 43)

The crucial problem of geopolitics for the European project is that it is primarily state-centric and rests on a simplistic, materialist-rationalist understanding of the national interest. For an EU returning to intergovernmentalism, geopolitics is not an abstract threat: a shift in world politics, such as the current multi-faceted crisis, can "stir up geopolitical discourses." (Guzzini & Leander, 2006, p. 13)

This historical potential for shifts towards geopolitical tendencies as a form of national foreign policies can be used as the negative scenario contrasted with a European, integrated view of foreign policy. Though an extreme scenario, a geopolitical Europe highlights the issue of a stand-alone European FPA argument: do EU big states rely on a more traditional foreign policy? Is a change visible? Is a reversal visible? A return to geopolitics can be modeled through two stages. First, a foreign policy discourse or tradition experiences an identity crisis when the unproblematic continuation of its interpretative disposition encounters problems, and taken-for-granted self-understandings and role positions are openly challenged, and eventually undermined. In the early 1990s, this crisis was induced by an external shock, the end of the Cold War. In current European politics, the trigger is a composite crisis that includes the economic and political challenges to the European project. (Balázs, 2014) Such a challenge is more likely to revive geopolitical thought when at least some of the following factors apply: a materialist tradition of thinking in foreign policy, the institutionalization of such a tradition within the foreign policy expert culture, and a political game where such thought is rhetorically used for political gain.

The Guzzini volume's theoretical framework relies on Weldes' concept of "security imaginary" which is defined as a "structure of well-established meanings and social relations out of which representations about the world of international relations are created." (Guzzini & Leander, 2006, p. 52; cf. Weldes, 1999) In the process of representation and interpretation of international affairs, actors mobilize this reservoir of raw meanings embedded in the collective memory of the expert field, including historical scripts and analogies (what Weldes calls "articulation"), together with the embedded subject-position of a country in the international system ("interpellation"). This does not imply that there is only one way of looking at a country's role in the world, but rather that "there are shared features in the ways that debates about the past are conducted, or in the potential roles of a country in the world that can be conceived of." (Guzzini, 2013, p. 52) The terms foreign policy tradition and "security imaginary" are used interchangeably.

A foreign policy imaginary does not produce a single opinion, it always contains various scripts and subject positions, and different actors weigh these along different lines. A foreign policy tradition, rather than containing a readily applicable toolkit, allows debates on foreign policy to happen in the first place since it "defines the stakes, draws the boundaries of relevant/competent debate and ensures that people speak the same language when they dispute each others' points." (Guzzini, 2013, p. 53) A foreign policy tradition therefore can be thought of as a system of references that frames and authorizes certain opinions while discrediting others within a debate. Even though foreign policy-makers will disagree on certain issues, they do so within the terms which are already agreed upon within the intersubjectively shared foreign policy field of meanings. The prevalent subject positions within a state's foreign policy tradition will provide the basis for interpreting foreign policy events, and will only be overruled in special cases, when a given event is truly unexpected or produces a large anomaly, such as the end of the Cold War, or arguably the current political crisis in Europe. (Guzzini & Leander, 2006, pp. 54–55)

Building on Weldes' theory, the present analysis is by no means deterministic: the current crisis might give rise to several interpretations of national and European foreign policy roles other than those associated with geopolitics. Geopolitics is one of the more pessimistic scenarios, though, as it by definition weakens the European level with its state-centrism. Nevertheless, similarities between the two scenarios necessitate a reinterpretation of European foreign policy analysis, lately also bogged down by the overly theoretical conception of normative, global European actorness. Looking at available foreign policy traditions can give us an idea about how individual member states may interpret and attempt to solve the current pseudo-identity crisis. Since leadership is of crucial importance, its manifestations in the traditions that characterize large member states should be the focus of any analysis.

A foreign (security) imaginary/tradition is a discursive practice, as both Weldes (1999) and Guzzini (2013) demonstrate. This means that it cannot be understood independently of its "enactment." This enactment of the language of foreign policy can be traced in three connected but different settings: within the government or political system; within the media, schools and cultural institutions; and within the expert system of private or public think tanks, research institutes and universities of a given country. (Guzzini, 2013, p. 55) A crisis in this framework involves a misfit between the significance of a certain event and the subject-positions or roles that are embedded in a foreign policy imaginary. Since facts are often underdetermined by theory, Guzzini argues, several interpretations are feasible and therefore no dissonance among them prompted by the event itself need appear. For a crisis to actually occur, interpretations given to the event must be so that role conceptions are no longer self-evident. Identities flow naturally, but as soon as they need to justify their existence and assumptions, they are in a crisis. Research on foreign policy imaginaries should therefore start with a demand for an identity fixing, Guzzini et al. argue, not with the solution of an identity crisis. (Guzzini, 2013, pp. 55–56) Applied to the case of the political crisis in Europe, signs of an identity crisis are indeed visible. Where it will take European foreign policy and the EU as a global actor, will undoubtedly be a hotly debated topic in academic circles. Without necessarily getting into the resolution of such a debate, in the following section I propose an analytical framework that can be applied to these questions, specifically to the issue of potential shifts in the Big Three's foreign policy imaginaries.

A framework for analyzing leaderless Europe

How do we interpret the effects of a European identity crisis? Where is the CFSP headed? Such questions have traditionally been assessed through the toolkit of foreign policy analysis. From the IR point of view, the question is whether a distinct foreign policy is needed for Europe, *or*, since Europe is not a stand-alone actor, whether a combination of intergovernmentalism and state-level FPA is more suited for the task. Despite the obvious importance of large states in defining what goes under the umbrella of European foreign policy, a simple return to state-level foreign policy tools would be premature due to the aforementioned reflexive mechanism of Europeanization. Socialization within the European Union, and especially within the CFSP/ESDP, has shaped foreign policy identities. Despite the intergovernmental nature of foreign policy decisions, Europeanization has had an effect on how member states view international events and actions. To what extent one needs to take this European element seriously in investigating the future of European foreign policy and the role of large states is an additional question of this section.

Foreign policy analysis, the sub-discipline designed to investigate governmental foreign policy decisions, investigates

> the motives and other sources of the behavior of international actors, particularly states (…) by giving a good deal of attention to decision-making, initially so as to probe behind the formal self-description (and fictions) of the processes of government and public administration. (Hill, 2003, p. 10)

This oft-quoted definition of FPA also highlights a problem specific to European foreign policy: Hill argues that FPA is the analysis of the external relations of all independent actors in world politics, though he usually takes "actors" to mean the state. This is again the starting point of the central question for scholars of EU foreign policy: can the EU be seen as an independent actor in IR? Also, how should the foreign policies of EU member states be analyzed?

The widespread claim about the *sui generis* nature of the European Union had its impact on FPA as scholars called for a distinct approach to analyzing foreign policy in Europe. Though calls for a markedly European FPA are frequent in the literature, the criteria for judging the need for a new approach are underspecified. To remedy this problem, Larsen (2009) puts forward three separate interpretations of European FPA, arguing that their case-by-case use for the analysis of the national foreign policies of individual EU member states depends on the policy area under scrutiny. Foreign policy encompasses a wide range of policy issues, and Europeanization affects these fields to different degrees.

Here it is crucial to emphasize that the failure of European foreign policy and the ineffectiveness of the EEAS do not do away with the relevance of the European level in foreign policy matters. Despite the lack of coherent actorness, large-scale foreign policy activity can indeed be identified at the European level in various policy fields, ranging from trade to fishing and foreign aid. Therefore, *how* member state foreign policies can be analyzed within the EU framework also remains an important question: if we can identify foreign policy activity on the European level, then how does this affect foreign policies on the national level? Is it still viable to talk about a *national* foreign policy as FPA does? Or do EU member states constitute a separate category of states that requires its own FPA? This is an interesting theoretical and empirical challenge as size and foreign policy culture vary greatly among member states, and some level of variance can even be detected among policy areas.

In order to engage these issues, scholars of European foreign policy analysis combine traditional approaches to FPA with the ever growing literature on Europeanization to understand the interaction and links between the supranational (European) and national levels in foreign policy making. The recent body of works that the present analysis relies on continues the tradition of a European approach to foreign policy analysis that was pioneered by White

(1999), while also being attentive to the weakening normative power argument. (See Aggestam, 2008) This particular approach is sensitive to the environment in which national foreign policies are made, i.e. the EU itself, linking FPA and Europeanization. As I mentioned previously, Europeanization originally entailed the emergence of structures of governance at the European level, and was then expanded to investigate the top-down effects of said structures of integration on member state policies, as well as member state adaptation to the EU context. Foreign policy has never been a particularly well-researched topic of Europeanization for a number of reasons (Green Cowles, Caporaso, & Risse, 2001), but primarily because of the CFSP's special nature as a strongly intergovernmental element. Since states were the primary movers of foreign policy, the effects of the European level could well be filtered by state capitals so that they had a limited impact on domestic choices. (Hix & Goetz, 2000) This seemed to minimize the importance of the "goodness of fit" argument (see e.g. Larsen, 2009), i.e. the adjustment of national policies to EU-level policies and requirements. Therefore, the argument went, fewer competences are transferred to the European level in foreign policy than in other policy fields.[11]

Some works, such as Bulmer and Radaelli's (2004) analysis, have shown that Europeanization varies across policy fields even within the pre-2009 first pillar, meaning that the distinction does not necessarily lie between foreign policy and other fields. Nevertheless, analysts still have to account for the fact that foreign policy differs fundamentally from other policy fields (see e.g. Gross, 2011; Larsen, 2009): there is no vertical "chain of command" through which EU policy reaches a member state. (Bulmer & Radaelli, 2004, p. 9) Member states themselves usually devise EU policy on a consensual, yet ad hoc basis. Consequently, pressures are milder than in other policy fields. But all this does not mean that the effects of Europeanization are insignificant when it comes to foreign policy.

Europeanization is a reflexive process: it is not only about EU-level integration structures and their effects on state policies, but also about state responses to these supranational institutions and processes – to use a more contemporary metaphor, the "uploading" of national preferences and "downloading" of EU policy. In policy fields where member states retain much of their authority, the feedback loop seems even more crucial for understanding Europeanization. Yet the scope of this analysis does not allow for theorizing the role of the usual distinction between bottom-up and top-down effects of Europeanization, and the mechanisms of both processes. Rather, I would like to highlight the specificities of foreign policy.

"Uploading" refers to the construction of EU foreign policy, traditionally conceived through intergovernmental bargaining, where the European (common) position mostly represents the lowest common denominator after preference aggregation. (Moravcsik, 1993) From the point of view of rational institutionalism/liberal intergovernmentalism, foreign policy cooperation is seen as an instrument that enables states to pursue their goals more successfully and achieve more visibility globally than their own position would merit: the pooling of resources results in a "politics of scale effect." (Ginsberg, 1989) This mechanism also reinforces states' incentives to push their own preferences onto the EU level, provided EU foreign policy structures are working effectively and/or there are no clear alternatives.

---

11 This position reflects the argument that foreign policy is special, an element of state sovereignty that states are not willing to give up. In other words, the EU is primarily an economic project, not a political federation.

The EU channel is very lucrative when states cannot rely on unilateral action or when states seek to externalize national problems, for instance France's lobbying for the Mediterranean Partnership and presenting the Arab Spring as an all-European issue in 2010. (Mikail, 2011)

With different foreign policy traditions and instruments, the degree of foreign policy adaptation differs from state to state. Domestic factors, such as the size of the state, its foreign policy network, its national identity (e.g. Britain's traditional Euroscepticism) and strategic culture (Johnston, 1995) modify and shape Europeanization processes. Large states such as the Big Three are frequently portrayed as shapers of EU foreign policy (de Flers & Müller, 2012; Gross, 2011), but the impact on smaller states is more extensive in certain fields, for example aid policy.[12] (Tonra, 2000)

Despite a certain variance in analysts' positions, the general consensus is that there is an ongoing Europeanization process, the intensity of which changes across states and policy areas. (Risse, 2001) With foreign policy the question then becomes whether we need a distinct European version of foreign policy analysis, given the ongoing Europeanization of this area. Larsen (2009) identifies two extreme positions. At the one end, White (2001) claims that no new European FPA is needed. Manners and Whitman (2000), at the other end, maintain that a completely new FPA is needed to investigate the foreign policies of EU member states. Larsen challenges both extremes and claims that "the main criterion for whether a particular approach to FPA is required is the extent to which national foreign policy is conducted within the EU." (Larsen, 2009, p. 538) He, therefore, investigates not the impact of Europeanization on national foreign policies – which is of course common for the existing literature – but how foreign policies are conducted within the EU. This issue is heavily under-researched in the literature, so Larsen's explorative article represents a major leap forward. Given the ongoing "silent revolution," the issues investigated within it will dominate the future of member states' foreign policies and the incorporation of the European element.

Larsen introduces three versions of foreign policy "lenses" that can be applied on a case-by-case basis to assess the foreign policies of European states: traditional, postmodern and transformed. Whereas the existing literature focuses on national approaches to the CFSP, as well as on its limits and possibilities that are shaped by national positions, recent analyses shift the focus to the effects of European foreign policy on national foreign policies. Two recent works deal with this. Brian White's *Understanding European Foreign Policy* (2001) distinguishes three kinds of foreign policies: community foreign policies that fall under the jurisdiction of the European Commission, for instance trade or development; the Common Foreign and Security Policy; and national foreign policies. These subsystems of European foreign policy governance are linked, White argues, and show that national foreign policies can be separated analytically for the purposes of foreign policy analysis, yet the European level should still be taken into account. The second book is Ben Tonra's *The Europeanization of National Foreign Policy: Dutch, Danish and Irish Foreign Policy in the European Union* (2001), in which he argues that there are mechanisms at work within the CFSP that challenge the common (intergovernmental) foreign policy model used by a number of analysts in relation to analyses of states' foreign policy in an EU context. In a similar fashion, White (2001) finds

---

12   As Larsen (2009) shows, the impact of EU policy on national foreign policies varies considerably across issue areas: there are some issue areas where certain small states may overshadow their large counterparts.

that there are meaning structures at work that concern European decision-making procedures which give the EU a central role in national foreign policy, especially with small states. He thus suggests a wide-ranging Europeanization of national foreign policies. The bottom line for Tonra is that national foreign policy making is more endogenous to the EU context than previously theorized. He shows a national adherence to European norms and rules in terms of foreign policy that goes beyond formal unanimity rules in the CFSP. Therefore, he maintains, a distinct European FPA is needed.

A third important contribution to the Europeanization debate in FPA is Manners and Whitman's *The Foreign Policy of European Union Member States* (2000), where the authors also argue for a distinct European FPA, suggesting a framework of comparative analysis of EU member states' foreign policies consisting of three categories: 1) foreign policy change (adaptation and socialization); 2) foreign policy process (domestic and bureaucratic); and 3) foreign policy action (whether it takes place with or without the EU). Based on the empirical testing of this framework, Whitman and Manners conclude that a new FPA, distinctively European and understood as pluralistic as opposed to national, needs to be adopted. The central question one can take away from the Manners-Whitman book, Larsen argues, is whether European foreign policy elites have been socialized into cooperative EU structures. Yet the book does not deal with the connection between socialization in EU structures and the effect of such socialization on national foreign policies. Nevertheless, such a connection is possible and would have a visible imprint on national foreign policy imaginaries, facilitating a national, but still markedly European, foreign policy for key member states. Taken together for the purposes of the present analysis, all three works highlight the need for a distinct European FPA despite the lack of a *de facto* common European foreign policy and the growing threat of foreign policy re-nationalization.

The existence of counteracting trends does not invalidate a European understanding of foreign policy analysis: EU foreign policy and member state foreign policy are both parts of EU foreign policy governance, but can be separated analytically. (See White, 2001, p. 39) Thus the two do not have to be mutually exclusive: EU foreign policy does not have to fully overtake national foreign policies to be meaningful. It is the interaction between the two elements that will decide whether a distinct European FPA is necessary. Following this logic, two extremes can be sketched. One is where foreign policy is conducted with the EU as just one of the elements of the state's foreign policy environment. The state conducts its foreign policy with many other partners, including other international organizations such as the World Bank or the United Nations. Here, a relatively autonomous formation of preferences can be assumed, which is then promoted on the international scene. This interpretation of foreign policy making falls close to liberal intergovernmentalism as conceptualized by Andrew Moravcsik (1993), and fits the toolkit of traditional FPA. At the other extreme, if all functional and geographical areas towards which the state directs its foreign policy are dealt with through one specific organization, the EU, then traditional FPA is fundamentally challenged. In this interpretation, EU foreign policy and national foreign policy can be conceptualized as concentric spheres, as "a shell around a shell." (Larsen, 2009, p. 544) This means that for the member state, the international environment is mediated through an organizational context: states interpret and respond to this context via the EU. National foreign policy concepts are heavily influenced by European foreign policy and the analysis of the EU's foreign policy-making process overtakes, or at least is coupled with, the analysis of national foreign policy-making processes.

The question analysts should ask themselves is when to use which approach. If the case in question is closer to the traditional, nation state-centric endpoint, then a foreign policy analysis will not bear too many European characteristics. In other situations where competences are shared or are exclusively supranational (the Community has exclusive legal competence over fishing and trade, for instance), a European approach is necessary. Thus, it is obvious that the choice of FPA approaches can vary across policy areas, but also across states as some states are more likely to enact certain policies through the EU than others. A useful rule of thumb for the analysis of national foreign policies, then, can be broken down into three steps:

1) *Where?* Where (in which fora, with which partners) does the state conduct its foreign policy? Does it do so primarily, partly or not at all through the EU?
2) *Why?* The background of the previous question tells us which elements to take into account in an empirical analysis. Though it is difficult to establish a "generic" member state due to variation in history, culture, size, etc., the Big Three should be the primary focus of future analyses.
3) *Is there a "Fit"?* National policies are not launched in a vacuum, but EU foreign policy does not affect national policies necessarily *a priori* either. Different areas lead to different degrees of policy outside or inside the EU. The EU is an obvious starting point with any area, given the comprehensive character of its policy framework. If an EU position is missing, states with established foreign policy frameworks still have an easier time looking for alternatives than states that surrendered the majority of their foreign policy to the EU.

Two dimensions reflect the context of foreign policy for member states: the EU position, and the assertions of national agency. With regards to the EU position, the presence of an EU foreign policy is a prerequisite for the whole argument to work. If a common European position and subsequent policy does not exist and cannot be created, then states fall back on national foreign policies. And if we follow Guzzini et al.'s (2013) logic, these national policies may very well weaken the EU, limiting the possibility of a common policy ever seeing the light of day. Looking at existing EU policies, they fall between two extremes. At one end, policies are detailed, resourceful and long-term with day-to-day involvement and a number of tools. At the other end they are based on few resources and only involve general statements. This variation may have a geographical element, e.g. EU policies towards the Balkans or the Eastern partnership are more robust than those geared towards Africa or Oceania. The geographical focus also affects individual member states to different degrees. While Eastern member states have a vested interest in the Eastern Partnership, France has always had a Mediterranean focus. Links to these regions can facilitate politics outside of the EU, while a lack of such links gives an incentive to follow the EU position.

It is important to emphasize that the EU framework differs from the framework of other international organizations because it encompasses a wider range of policy areas. In addition, with the EU, foreign policy making forms part of a more general, deep integration process (federalism) that compromises the policy-making structures of all member states. Therefore all states consider the EU as important for their foreign policies on a general level, even the big ones. Thus, to reiterate, the lack of an EU foreign policy does not limit the instrumental use of the EU for self-representation, however, it casts a shadow over the need for a markedly European FPA. This point is supported by the argument that EU foreign policy is the result of state action so it can be weakened if the states so choose. (Larsen, 2009, p. 550)

In line with the assumptions about the foreign policy identity and role conceptions of states, the framework of meaning within which national policy is shaped is viewed as the fundamental structural factor in the domestic realm, shaping and constraining other forces. Who we are defines what we should and can do. The crucial question is who the "we" is in particular policy areas – the state, the EU or a combination of both? – and what the content, characteristics and goals of this "we" are. Countries' understanding of their role in different geographical and policy areas differs widely. Large states are generally more engaged and more assertive in a range of areas, both physical and policy, as exemplified by the role identity of a "responsible power." (Rosenthal, 1991) Small states, on the other hand, are more engaged in their immediate neighborhood and favor more symbolic and/or crucial policy areas, such as aid policy for Nordic states, or the integration of the Western Balkans for Hungary. In other areas, small states are more likely to act as followers of either an organization like the EU, a larger state, or a coalition of states.

Thus the articulated agency (the "we") does not have to be a national we, it can incorporate the EU, thereby blurring the national character of foreign policy. At least four possibilities can be imagined: just the country; just the EU; the country and the EU; or the EU presented as an essential part of the construction, i.e. acting through the EU. (Larsen, 2009, p. 552) Based on the possible archetypes of EU policy strength, four modes can be sketched, which are also represented in Table 1:

- *Mode 1*: EU Foreign Policy is Intensive and Resourceful; Little Articulation of National Agency
- *Mode 2*: EU Foreign Policy is Not Intensive or Resourceful; Little Articulation of National Agency
- *Mode 3*: EU Foreign is Policy Intensive and Resourceful; National Articulation of Agency
- *Mode 4*: EU Foreign Policy is Not Intensive and Resourceful; National Articulation of Agency

Table 1. Four modes of conducting foreign policy

	EU Foreign Policy Intensive and Resourceful	EU Foreign Policy Not Intensive and Resourceful
Little Articulation of National Agency	Little national foreign policy conducted outside of the EU (1)	National foreign policy? (2)
Articulation of National Agency	National foreign policy conducted inside and outside of the EU (3)	National foreign policy mainly conducted outside of the EU (4)

Source: Larsen (2009, p. 555).

A transformed FPA is especially needed in Mode 1. However, this combination of types usually does not apply to big states in most areas. Articulation of joint agency here would point to a strong European effect on national policies. Most importantly this applies to issue areas covered exclusively by the Commission. Mode 2 is weak on both scales, it has little "national" or "European" in it. Questions that are crucial for the future of the CFSP fall outside of this mode. Mode 3 on the other hand calls for a "postmodern FPA," in which national foreign policy could be seen as part of a foreign policy system where both the EU and the state are significant international actors. (Larsen, 2009; see Ruggie, 1993 on postmodernity and IR) In Mode 3, analysts will have to take into account decision-making procedures in the EU when assessing national foreign policy, since the EU is considered a crucial forum in foreign policy making. This mode applies to policy areas where CFSP integration is advanced, and to states that subvert their – nonetheless articulated – national foreign policy identities to Europeanization. Here it is also necessary to include traditional concerns about the international environment containing other states and institutional actors. Therefore, as Larson argues, we will need a double analysis. Finally, Mode 4 sees little activity on the European level with a strong articulation of national agency, thereby inviting a traditional FPA approach. Out of these possibilities, Modes 3 and 4 apply most to big states, and Larsen himself admits that the foreign policy of large member states will often be closer to the traditional lens. (Larsen, 2009, p. 559) Relying on these archetypes of member state foreign policies enables a structured analysis of large EU state foreign policies, which in turn enables analysts and policy-makers to assess where European foreign policy might be headed. Current crises, such as the Russian invasion of the Crimean Peninsula and the Eastern Ukrainian crisis, put more and more pressure on the EU as a supposedly unified actor. A careful, theoretically informed investigation of member state foreign policy imaginaries may help in navigating such situations.

Conclusion: adaptation pressures

The ongoing political, economic and legitimacy crisis of the EU shows that the Europeanization of foreign policy can indeed be reversed through a process of re-nationalization of policy competences. EU member states may very well fall back on their own resources and individual strategies to help manage political crises outside of the confines of European regulations. De-Europeanization could also occur after changes in government if domestic actors who oppose EU-inspired changes are empowered, just as we could see with the Cameron government in the United Kingdom, or with the foreign policy realignment of the Hungarian government under Viktor Orbán. Foreign policy is still a highly symbolic, elite policy issue area that states are reluctant to surrender. A general feeling of Euroscepticism thus might induce changes in national stances on foreign policy matters. These changes often do not carry much political risk domestically, yet are still symbolic, and can therefore be used as an eurosceptic "show of force:" politicians can easily argue that they renationalize foreign policy, one of the cornerstones of national sovereignty. But practical reasons can also motivate a de-Europeanization in terms of foreign policy if a state perceives the EU as acting against its narrowly conceived state interest, or if the EU fails to appear as a deciding actor in matters important to the member state in question.

The current political problem is of course that the crisis heightens the importance of such moves for both symbolic and pragmatic reasons. For example, calling for sanctions against Russia on the European level can be seen in some capitals as detrimental to their interest. As de Flers and Müller rightly argue, a working European common foreign policy is not only about the socialization of national representatives within EU bodies, but also a gradual learning process, for instance through reaction to crises such as the 2003 Iraq war.

(de Flers and Müller, 2012, p. 28) The current international situation puts EU foreign policy under a series of interrelated stress tests, which often imply conflicting policy decisions. (Balázs, 2014) For example, three classic, potentially conflicting commitments are surfacing in connection with the Eurozone crisis, Ukraine or the Snowden affair: national interest, transatlantic relations (NATO and United States bilateral), and European commitments. How states manage the potential friction among the three commitments and when and where they prefer the EU channel will be one of the key topics of European foreign policy. Using the theoretical framework I offer in this chapter, and focusing on states that will have a key role in deciding the future of the CFSP, analysts can better assess how a leaderless European Union can cope with a turbulent new world and a "wider Europe" in flux.

Bibliography

Aggestam, L. (2008). Introduction: Ethical Power Europe? *International Affairs*. 84(1), 1–10.

Allen, D., & Smith, M. (1990). Western Europe's Presence in the Contemporary International Arena. *Review of International Studies*. 16(1), 19–37.

Allison, G. T. (1972). Bureaucratic Politics: A Paradigm and Some Policy Implications. *World Politics*. 24, 40-79.

Balázs, P. (Ed.). (2014). *Europe's Position in the New World Order*. Budapest: CEU Center for EU Enlargement Studies.

Bickerton, C. J. (2013). *European Integration: From Nation-States to Member States*. Oxford: Oxford University Press.

Bulmer, S., & Radaelli, C. M. (2004). The Europeanisation of National Policy? (Queen's Paper on Europeanisation No. 1/2004). Retrieved from http://www.qub.ac.uk/schools/SchoolofPoliticsInternationalStudiesandPhilosophy/FileStore/EuropeanisationFiles/Filetoupload,38405,en.pdf. Visited 23.09.2014

Buras, P. (2013). The EU's Silent Revolution. European Council on Foreign Relations. Retrieved from http://www.ecfr.eu/page/-/ECFR87_EU_SILENT_REVOLU-TION_AW.pdf. Visited 23.09.2014

De Flers, N. A., & Müller, P. (2012). Dimensions and Mechanisms of the Europeanization of Member State Foreign Policy: State of the Art and New Research Avenues. *Journal of European Integration*. 34(1), 19–35.

Drezner, D. W. (2000). Ideas, Bureaucratic Politics, and the Crafting of Foreign Policy. *American Journal of Political Science*. 44(4), 733–749.

Elgström, O., & Smith, M. (2006). *The European Union's Roles in International Politics: Concepts and Analysis*. New York: Routledge.

European Security Strategy: A Secure Europe in a Better World. (2003). Brussels: European Council.

Fligstein, N., Polyakova, A., & Sandholtz, W. (2012). European Integration, Nationalism and European Identity. *Journal of Common Market Studies*. 50(1), 106–122.

Ginsberg, R. H. (1989). *Foreign Policy Actions of the European Community: The Politics of Scale*. Boulder: Lynne Rienner.

Ginsberg, R. H. (1999). Conceptualizing the European Union as an International Actor: Narrowing the Theoretical Capability-Expectations Gap. Pittsburgh. Retrieved from http://aei.pitt.edu/2275/1/002630.PDF. Visited 24.09.2014.

Green Cowles, M., Caporaso, J. A., & Risse, T. (Eds.). (2001). *Transforming Europe: Europeanization and Domestic Change*. Ithaca: Cornell University Press.

Gross, E. (2011). *The Europeanization of National Foreign Policy: Continuity and Change in European Crisis Management*. Basingstoke: Palgrave.

Guzzini, S. (Ed.). (2013). *The Return of Geopolitics in Europe?: Social Mechanisms and Foreign Policy Identity Crises*. Cambridge: Cambridge University Press.

Guzzini, S., & Leander, A. (Eds.). (2006). *Constructivism and International Relations: Alexander Wendt and His Critics*. New York: Routledge.

Hill, C. (1993). The Capability-Expectations Gap, or Conceptualizing Europe's International Role. *Journal of Common Market Studies*. 31(3), 305–328.

Hill, C. (2003). *The Changing Politics of Foreign Policy*. New York: Palgrave.

Hix, S., & Goetz, K. H. (Eds.). (2000). *Europeanised Politics? European Integration and National Political Systems*. London: Routledge.

Hyde-Price, A. (2006). Normative power Europe: A realist critique. *Journal of European Public Policy*. 13(2), 217–234.

Johnston, I. A. (1995). Thinking about Strategic Culture. *International Security*. 19(4), 32–64.

Jørgensen, K. (2004). European Foreign Policy: Conceptualising the Domain. In W. Carlsnaes, B. White, & H. Sjursen (Eds.), *Contemporary European Foreign Policy*. London: SAGE.

Jupille, J., & Caporaso, J. A. (1998). States, Agency, and Rules: The European Union in Global Environmental Politics. In C. Rhodes (Ed.), *The European Union in the World Community*. Boulder: Lynne Rienner.

Larsen, H. (2002). The EU: A global military actor? *Cooperation and Conflict2*. 37(3), 283–302.

Larsen, H. (2009). A Distinct FPA for Europe? Towards a Comprehensive Framework for Analyzing the Foreign Policy of EU Member States. *European Journal of International Relations*. 15(3), 537–566.

Lucarelli, S., & Manners, I. (Eds.). (2006). *Values and Principles in European Union Foreign Policy*. New York: Routledge.

Lyon, G. (2010). Lady Ashton: Mistaking Quiet Diplomacy for Silence. *The Guardian*. Retrieved from http://www.theguardian.com/commentisfree/2010/jul/19/lady-ashton-silence-quiet-diplomacy

Manners, I. (2002). Normative power Europe: A contradiction in terms? *Journal of Common Market Studies*. 40(2), 235-258.

Manners, I. (2006). European Union "Normative Power" and the Security Challenge. *European Security*. 15(4), 405–421.

Manners, I. (2008). Normative Power Europe: A Transdisciplinary Approach to European Studies. In C. Rumford (Ed.), *Handbook of European Studies*. London: Sage Publications.

Manners, I., & Whitman, R. (2000). *The Foreign Policies of European Union Member States*. Manchester: Manchester University Press.

Manners, I., & Whitman, R. (2003). The 'Difference Engine': Constructing and Representing the International Identity of the European Union. *Journal of European Public Policy*. 10(3), 380-404.

Mikail, B. (2011). France and the Arab spring: an opportunistic quest for influence. (Working Paper No. 110), FRIDE. Retrieved from http://www.fride.org/download/wp110_france_and_arab_spring.pdf. Visited 13.09.2014.

Moravcsik, A. (1993). Preferences and Power in the European Community: A Liberal Intergovernmentalist Approach. *Journal of Common Market Studies*. 31(4), 473–524.

Moravcsik, A. (1999). Is Something Rotten in the State of Denmark? Constructivism and European Integration. *Journal of European Public Policy*. 6(4), 669–681.

Moravcsik, A. (2010). Europe: Rising Superpower in a Bipolar World. In A. S. Alexandroff & A. F. Cooper (Eds.), *Rising States, Rising Institutions: Challenges for Global Governance* (pp. 151–174). Washington DC: Brookings Institution Press.

Nye, J. S. (2004). *Soft power: The means to success in world politics*. New York: Public Affairs.

Nye, J. S. (2011). *The Future of Power*. New York: Perseus.

Radaelli, C. M. (2003). The Europeanization of Public Policy. In K. Featherstone & C. M. Radaelli (Eds.), *The Politics of Europeanization* (pp. 27–56). Oxford: Oxford University Press.

Risse, T. (2001). Who Are We? A Europeanization of National Identities? In M. Green Cowles & J. Caporaso (Eds.), *Transforming Europe* (pp. 198–216). Ithaca: Cornell University Press.

Rosencrance, R. (1998). "The European Union: A New Type of International Actor" in J. Zielonka (Ed.) *Paradoxes of European Foreign Policy* (pp.15-25). The Hague: Kluwer.

Rosenthal, J. H. (1991). *Righteous Realists: Political Realism, Responsible Power, and American Culture in the Nuclear Age*. Baton Rouge: Louisiana State University Press.

Ruggie, J. G. (1993). Territoriality and Beyond: Problematizing Modernity in International Relations. *International Organization*. 47(1), 139–174.

Solana, J. (2005). Speech on "Shaping an Effective EU Foreign Policy." Brussels: Konrad Adenauer Foundation.

Tonra, B. (2000). Mapping EU Foreign Policy. *Journal of European Public Policy*. 7(1).

Tonra, B. (2001). *The Europeanization of National Foreign Policy: Dutch, Danish and Irish Foreign Policy in the European Union*. New York: Ashgate.

Weldes, J. (1998). Bureaucratic Politics: A Critical Constructivist Assessment. *Mershon International Studies Review*. 42(2), 216–225.

Weldes, J. (1999). The Cultural Production of Crises: U.S. Identity and Missiles in Cuba. In J. Weldes, M. Laffey, H. Gusterson, & R. Duvall (Eds.), *Cultures of Insecurity: States, Communities, and the Production of Danger* (pp. 35–62). London: University of Minnesota Press.

White, B. (2001). *Understanding European Foreing Policy*. London: Palgrave.

Wong, R., & Hill, C. (Eds.). (2011). *National and European Foreign Policies*. New York: Routledge.

Wong, R. Y.-P. (2010). G-3?: Conceptualising a US-EU-China Triad in International Relation. Porto: ECPR 5th Pan-European Conference.

Zürn, M., & de Wilde, P. (2012). Can the Politicization of European Integration be Reversed? *Journal of Common Market Studies*. 50(1), 137–153.

THE EU AND INTERNATIONAL TRADE

KATALIN VARGA

This chapter analyzes the trade relationship between the European Union (EU) and its neighboring countries, while keeping in mind the book's overall goal, which is to determine how the global crisis has changed the EU's influence in the "wider Europe." Relations between the EU and its neighbors from the wider Europeare complex and include both political and economic dimensions. International trade relations are therefore only one of the means through which the EU can extend its influence to the neighboring countries. My aim here is to single out the effect of the trade sector from other segments of the cooperation between the EU and the partner countries. In order to do so, I have selected specific indicators that show different aspects of these trade ties. I first analyze quantitative measures, specifically the EU's share in the partner countries' exports and imports, because these highlight the relative trade power of the EU in these countries. Second, I analyze the trade agreements between the EU and the partner countries. The EU's approach to international trade has fundamentally changed in the last decade. While earlier the EU mainly participated in multilateral trade agreements, it has since then started to prioritize bilateral ones. This allows the EU to differentiate the conditions of its trade relations with individual countries. In our case, this means that the EU's trade agreements with its neighbors are diverse and qualitatively different and that they imply different levels of cooperation. In order to determine the integrative power of these agreements, I examine the depth of integration they represent.

The overall project's goal is to follow the consequences of the global crisis as it unfolds. In line with that, I concentrate in this chapter on the period after the start of the crisis (2007 – 2008) and up to 2013. This short time frame means that the conclusions to be drawn from the analysis, and the opportunities to develop forecasts based on the findings, can only be restricted. In order to compensate for the limitations of the time scale, the indicators are analyzed in the context of longer trends, allowing me to detect short-term changes that may have been caused by the global crisis.

The chapter aims to give a wide comparative overview regarding trade relations between the EU and its neighborhood. Hence, three fundamentally different cases are examined, namely Turkey, Ukraine and the Western Balkans. The quantitative indicators for the latter are presented separately for each country but are otherwise handled together in line with the EU's rather unified approach to these states. The analysis that follows is wide in its scope but with limitations as to its depth, as several possible aspects of the question will not be examined. An analysis of product types that the EU exports to and import from the partner countries can, for instance, give information about the symmetry of the relationship, but the framework of the current chapter does not allow for such a detailed investigation of the sectoral composition of the trade issues. Moreover, I will not analyze the text of the trade agreements in depth, because the main goal of this chapter is to provide the overall picture, not to give a detailed analysis regarding the individual cases.

This chapter aims to provide information to all audiences. I therefore concentrate on those aspects of trade relations that have important policy implications, leaving technical arguments aside.

The chapter is organized as follows: I first give an overview of some methodological issues, before analyzing the individual cases. I then give a comparative discussion before concluding the chapter.

Methodological overview

The goal of this analysis is two-fold: it aims, first, to assess the effects of the 2007 – 2009 crisis on trade relations between the EU and its neighboring countries, and, second, to examine whether the institutions connected to these trade relations are able to enhance the integration of the partner countries with the EU.

In the first part, I therefore seek to determine whether and to what extent the decline of the EU's economic power can be detected through analyzing its trade policy. Even though it is common knowledge that the EU's overall resources have considerably shrunk since 2007, a separate analysis is necessary in order to determine how much that spills over into the trade sector. Measuring the strength of trade connections is a highly delicate matter. Although detailed trade statistics are available regarding different layers of international trade even to the level of individual products, interpreting the numbers is far from straightforward. Measurement problems arise on all levels, which then make comparative analysis rather controversial. The present chapter does not allow for a detailed analysis of trade between the EU and its neighbors, but the project's focus is centered on macro-level issues such as integration and therefore does not prevent drawing the conclusions necessary to answer the research questions. In order to capture the dynamics of trade performance, I analyze both quantitative data and policy measures, because they encapsulate different aspects of trade relations. Using the quantitative data, I aim to establish whether the EU's position in its neighboring countries' trade volume has declined. This can help find out whether the EU's trade power has declined relative to other countries or regions since the global crisis. Hence, I analyze the EU's ratio in the foreign trade of Turkey, Ukraine and the Western Balkans in the seven-year time frame since 2007. Since the crisis had a negative effect on the economies of both the EU and the other countries under study, we can expect a short-term drop in the intensity of trade. Moreover, as described above, the natural expectation is that the EU's economic problems do make its economic power decrease. Hence, here we can expect a decrease in the EU's share in trade with neighboring countries. In order to deal with the limitations due to the short time frame, I compare the dynamics before and after 2007. Hence, I present the EU's share in the international trade of Turkey, Ukraine and the Western Balkans since 2000. Moreover, whenever possible I compare data from different sources in order to get a more balanced picture. However, I analyze not the absolute volume of trade but only the EU's relative share. The EU is still one of these countries' major economic partners. In case the overall trade performance of the given third country has increased since 2007, we will see growth in the volume of the trade between the EU and this country, even if the EU's share in the country's overall trade has declined. But the aim here is to establish whether the EU is losing power compared to these countries' other trading partners. This can be analyzed through an investigation of the relative position of the EU, meaning its proportion of the overall trade of these countries.

An alternative way to analyze changes in the strength of trade relations since the crisis is to look at trade policies and to examine how deep trade integration has become. The differentiation between shallow and deep integration was first formulated by Lawrence. (Lawrence, 1996) In his definition, shallow integration means the removal of border protection measures without regulatory coordination. This means that the most direct trade barriers, such as tariffs and some non-tariff barriers, are removed, but that there is no further coordination of policies. Traditionally, this has been the first and, for a long time, the only step towards trade liberalization. "Once tariffs are removed, complex problems remain because of differing regulatory policies among nations. Traditionally, such policies are determined and administered at the national level, according foreign goods and firms nondiscriminatory national treatment – an approach I have called shallow integration." (Ibid., p. 64) Hence, at this stage of trade relations where coordination is mostly limited to quantitative measures, institutional coordination remains highly superficial. That also implies that integration between the two countries remain superficial. In our case, shallow integration implies that the EU has limited influence in the given country. In contrast to this, deep integration means that, on top of the removal of border trade barriers, there is also regulatory approximation between the countries. This can include harmonization of regulations directly related to international trade, for instance production standards, sanitary requirements and other non-tariff barriers. (Evans, Holmes, Iacovone, & Robinson, 2004) However, this can be expanded to include other measurements which indirectly boost trade relations, such as policies to integrate production processes across national borders or help investment flows, which can help economic performance and through that also international trade performance itself. Moreover, it may also include measures that have long-term effects, and which support overall integration between countries and not only trade connections themselves, e.g. common institutions setting standards through dialogues between the two parties, harmonizing legal regulation of markets or regional development funds. This results in deeper integration between the partner countries. Here, deep integration means that the EU has greater influence in the partner country.

Simply put, in the current framework shallow integration means that the EU has weaker trade power and, deep integration that the EU has stronger trade power. Hence, it would be logical to expect that trade treaties between the EU and its neighbors have become shallower. However, the time that has elapsed since the crisis is not sufficient to expect such fundamental changes in the quality of trade relations. First of all, already existing trade agreements are very rarely reversed. Second, trade negotiations usually take years or even decades to conclude. This time frame is too short to expect that these trade agreements could considerably change, mostly because it was only after 2009 that policy makers started to understand the real extent of the crisis and were able to act in response. Hence, realistically the following can signal the EU's decreasing trade power: negotiations slowing down, future plans postponed or made looser. Since all these are incremental changes, it is important to note that any conclusion regarding the direction of these trade relationships will be based on personal judgment and should not be handled as clear predictions.

After determining whether the EU lost trade power either in quantitative or in qualitative terms, I seek to analyze whether trade institutions between the EU and its partner countries are such as to enhance the integration process. This is related to the depth of the integration. As explained earlier deeper integration means more interconnection, meaning that the EU has greater influence on the partner countries' internal structure. Deep integration is by default symmetrical, meaning that the countries entering into such cooperation can all influ-ence each other's rules, policies and institutions. However, in the case of the EU and its neighboring countries, we cannot speak about such reciprocity. The EU's approach to these countries is based on strict conditionality, meaning that the EU is willing to liberalize trade with these countries only if they correspond to the policy criteria set by the EU, criteria which include the adoption of diverse regulatory regimes and institutions. Hence, the influ-ence of the EU in the partner countries depends on these regulations and institutions. The more these are embedded in the overall economic and social structure of the country, the stronger the integration between the EU and the partner country. When analyzing the strength of the integration between the EU and the partner country, I therefore look at the regulatory and institutional requirements of the trade treaty. Nevertheless, it is important to note that this does not give us an overall picture regarding the integration of the EU and the partner country. In order to obtain that, aspects beyond trade also need to be analyzed, which are addressed in the other chapters of the present book. The focus here is on trade issues.

The analysis is structured in the following way for each country. First, based on the EU's weight in the overall foreign trade of a given country, I aim to determine whether the EU's economic problems have translated into more limited trade power. Second, based on the qualitative analysis of the trade policies and treaties, I aim to investigate changes in the depth of trading relations since 2007. Simply put, deeper integration means more possibilities for the transfer of EU institutions. Third, I aim to analyze whether the institutions related to trade are strong enough that the EU still has influence in these countries, taking this as a further indicator of the depth of trade integration.

Case studies

Turkey

From the point of view of the trade relationships between Turkey and the EU, it is highly important to note that Turkey's international trade situation has changed significantly in the last few years. Among other developments, the direction of imports and exports shows that the locus of trade is shifting away from the EU to other regions. (Babacan, 2011; Szigetvári, 2013a; World Trade Organisation Trade Policy Review Body, 2012) As can be seen from Figure 1, this has been a longer trend for imports than for exports. The EU's share in Tur-key's exports has been rather stable at around 56% - 58% until 2007, when within a year it dropped radically by 8.6 percentage points. After a further small decrease, it stabilized at around 46%, but dropped again radically in 2012. The EU's share in Turkey's exports has repeatedly declined since the start of the global crisis, to the extent that while before the crisis the EU accounted for more than 55% of Turkey's exports, in 2012 this was less than 40%. On the other hand, the EU's share in Turkey's imports has been decreasing since the beginning of the 2000s. Even though the trend was temporarily reversed several times dur-ing this period, it dropped from 52.4% in 2000 to 40.2% by 2007 and further to 37% by 2012. Nevertheless, the start of the global crisis seems not to have brought any change in the trend as the decline after 2008 was in line with earlier developments.

Figure 1. Turkey's main trading partners' share in Turkish foreign trade: long-term trends

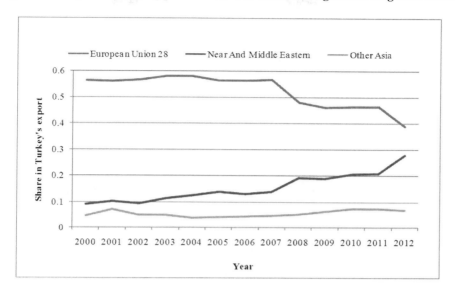

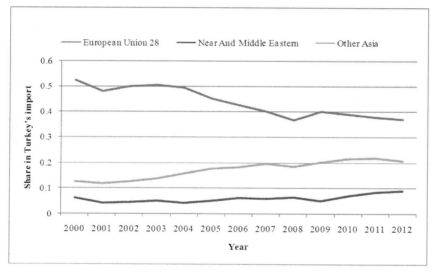

Source: Turkish Statistical Institute, 2013; own calculations.

In order to have a broader overview of the changes of the EU's share in Turkey's exports and imports, Table 1 presents the EU's share in the merchandise trade of Turkey based on two different sources (European Commission Directorate-General for Trade, 2013a; Turkish Statistical Institute, 2013). Even though the exact numbers are different, both time series show the same trend described above.

Table 1. Direction of Turkish merchandise trade with the EU

	EU's share of total exports	
	Turkstat data	EU data
2000	56.4%	
2001	56.1%	
2002	56.7%	
2003	58.1%	
2004	58.1%	
2005	56.5%	
2006	56.3%	
2007	56.7%	
2008	48.1%	39.1%
2009	46.1%	36.6%
2010	46.4%	37.1%
2011	46.4%	37.2%
2012	38.9%	29.3%

Source: European Commission Directorate-General for Trade, 2013; Turkish Statistical Institute, 2013; own calculations. The columns labeled Turkstat data show the share of EU28 in the Turkish exports and imports respectively, calculated by the author based on data from the Turkish Statistical Institute (2013). The columns labeled EU data show the EU's share in Turkish exports and imports respectively as presented by European Commission Directorate-General for Trade (2013a).

The trade relations between the EU and Turkey had already been loosening before the start of the global crisis and this has further accelerated since 2008. On the country level the trend is even more striking. Table 2 shows how EU member states have become less important for Turkey's trade compared to other countries. Nevertheless, it is important to note that this decrease has only happened in relative terms. The overall volume of exports and imports between Turkey and the EU has kept on growing even in the years when the EU's share in Turkish trade decreased. Moreover, the EU has remained Turkey's sole most important regional trade partner. (European Commission Directorate-General for Trade, 2013a; Szigetvári, 2013a)

Table 2. Ranking of Turkey's main trading partners in 2002 and 2012

Exports		
	2002	2012
1.	Germany	Germany
2.	USA	Iraq
3.	Great Britain	Iran
4.	Italy	Great Britain
5.	France	United Arab Emirates
6.	Russia	Russia
7.	Spain	Italy

Sources: Szigetvári, 2013a.
*The difference between Germany and China in the volume of imports towards Turkey was marginal in 2012 a nd China is expected to become Turkey's second largest import partner in 2013.

EU – Turkish trade relations have been guided by a Customs Union since the beginning of 1996. Its launch had a positive impact as the share of the EU in Turkey's trade increased, but this was due to trade diversion and not trade creation. (Ülgen & Zahariadis, 2004) Moreover, it had a structural effect on Turkey's economy, and through that contributed to the Turkish economic boom of the early 2000s. It opened up Turkey's markets to the world markets, meaning that Turkey had to increase its competitiveness. European markets became freely accessible for Turkish actors, which contributed to the development of traditional industries such as textiles. Moreover, as a result of the Customs Union, Turkey's production and export structure diversified and sectors other than textiles and agriculture also started to develop: several car companies, for instance, opened factories in Turkey and then built up the whole supply chain around the country. (Szigetvári, 2013a, 2013b)

However, Turkey's focus has in recent years started to shift to other regions. The main new actors for Turkish exports are the Middle Eastern countries, and for imports China and Russia. Export volume with Iran increased thirty-fold between 2002 and 2013 and to an even larger degree with Iraq. Moreover, the Middle Eastern countries are the only trading partners with which Turkey has a trade surplus. In addition to these destinations, Turkey is increasingly open-ing to Central Asia and the Balkans, where it starts to play a significant role in the construction industry. All in all, Turkey has been building up considerable soft power capabilities in its neighboring regions through trade relations. (Babacan, 2011; Szigetvári, 2012, 2013a)

The reasons behind this relative change in the EU's position in Turkish foreign trade are rather complex and are not only the result of declining demand from the EU. First, Turkey has become highly dependent on imports, mostly in energy. These come mostly from Russia, China and the Gulf countries, increasing the importance of these countries in Turkish im-ports. Second, Iraq is a completely new actor in this regard, as the trade embargo was only lifted in 2003. (N. Rózsa, 2013; Szigetvári, 2013b) Moreover, the Customs Union itself has structural weaknesses. When Turkey signed the agreement, it accepted all of the EU's exter-nal tariffs and trade agreements. This meant that Turkey also agreed to adhere to all the free trade agreements (FTAs) that the EU concludes with third parties. However, this is a one-sided act for Turkey, as even though Turkey needs to open its markets to the products of the third countries involved, these countries do not need to do the same, unless the EU is willing to add a "Turkish clause" to the agreements or the third country involved is willing to sign a separate agreement with Turkey. Opening its market in such an asymmetrical man-ner has already caused some problems for Turkey's trade, but serious problems started to emerge after the EU concluded FTAs with major countries such as Japan, South Korea or the USA, which do not intend to accept Turkish goods even though Turkey needs to accept their goods without any restrictions. (Babacan, 2011; McNamara, Cohen, & Phillips, 2010; Szigetvári, 2013b; Ülgen & Zahariadis, 2004) Hence, the Customs Union forced Turkey into a position where it has to adhere to decisions that it cannot influence.

Based on the above, the EU's influence in Turkey through trade relations can be charac-terized as follows. When concluding the Customs Union, Turkey needed to adopt the Euro-pean Community's legislation in several fields. This was a substantial regulatory alignment, which deepened integration between the EU and Turkey. (Ülgen & Zahariadis, 2004) Nev-ertheless the institutional transfer has not continued after the Customs Union. Moreover, as the EU's relative share in Turkey's international trade is decreasing, so is its influence through this channel. As described earlier, this can only partly be related to the global crisis as the decrease in the share of imports started earlier. Even though the EU has been losing weight in Turkey's trade only in relative terms, this change has been considerable. The share of the EU in Turkish exports has decreased by 32% from 2007 to 2012, and in imports by 30%

over a longer time period. The EU used to account for more than half of both exports and imports; these went down to less than 40% in both cases. In the case of imports the trend is a long-term one, and we can assume that it will continue because it derives from economic structural reasons, namely the EU's inability to satisfy certain needs in Turkey's developing industry. Since Turkey is highly dependent on imports, the fact that the EU's share is decreasing can have a considerable effect on its power even in non-trade related issues. In the case of exports the decline started with the global crisis. Hence, the time period has been too short to establish the extent and the influence of this trend.

Even though we can clearly talk about the decline of the EU's influence in Turkey through trade, it is important to note that this was not the only and probably not the most important channel of the EU's influence. The EU's decreasing share and the problems with the Customs Union agreement add to the other political problems between Turkey and the EU, such as the ever-pending accession negotiations – which are blocked again and again by the biggest EU member states, Cyprus, and visa liberalization. (Akçalı, 2013; Akgün, 2013; Tófalvi, 2014) Moreover, Turkey's ruling Justice and Development Party (AKP) has been using the nationalist argument, centered on the idea that Turkey is a "rising star" that is becoming a soft power in the region, as well as anti-EU ideas to polarize society, fight uprisings and secure its share of voters. (Akçalı, 2013) The high degree of politicization of the EU issue in Turkey can actually can have a stronger effect on the EU's possible influence than trade relations.

Ukraine

Ukraine is an interesting case as it also aspires to EU membership despite not yet having signed an Accession Agreement (AA) with the EU nor having as clear an association promise as Turkey. Figure 2 shows the changes in the volume of trade between the EU and Ukraine in the last decade, with differing trends for exports and imports.[1] The share of exports towards the EU started to decline in 2003 and by 2008 it went down to the extent that Ukraine's other biggest trading partners, in the region of the Commonwealth of Independent States (CIS), became relatively stronger than the EU. This trend was slightly reversed after the start of the global crisis in 2007. The EU's share in Ukraine's imports has always been smaller than that of the CIS countries, but the composition of imports from the two regions is completely different; "Ukraine imports high value-added products from the EU and energy resources from the CIS countries (mostly Russia)." (Dabrowski & Taran, 2012, p. 9) The EU's share in Ukraine's imports grew between 2000 and 2007 by around 10 percentage points before switching to a continued decrease after the start of the global crisis. All in all, we can see that the 2007 crisis has only had a minor effect on the different partners' shares in Ukraine's trade volume.

---

1   The data presented in these two figures come from two different sources, hence the discrepancy between the two trend lines describing the EU's share

Figure 2. The EU's share in Ukraine's foreign trade: long-term trends

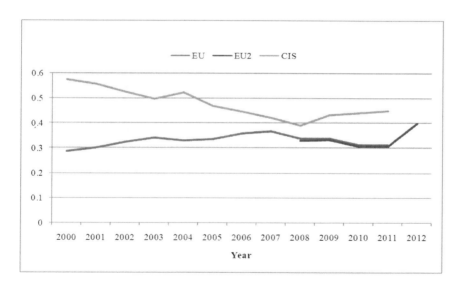

Source: For data labeled EU and CIS: Dabrowski & Taran, 2012; for data labeled EU2: European Commission Directorate-General for Trade, 2013b.

The trade relationship between Ukraine and the EU has been regulated by the Generalised Scheme of Preferences (GSP) since 1993 (European Commission, 2013a) and the more general Partnership and Cooperation Agreement (PCA) signed in June 1994. The PCA does not offer strong enough incentives for the partner countries to harmonize their regulation and institutional setup. Moreover, the PCA in force with Ukraine does not contain preferential treatment for trade or other extensive bilateral trade measures, except for the provisions related to World Trade Organization (WTO) measures, for instance the Most Favored Nation (MFN) clause (*Partnership and Cooperation Agreement between the European Communities and their Member States, and Ukraine*, 1998), which both parties had to implement because they are members of the WTO. The GSP, on the other hand, is a clear trade arrangement. Because of its income level, Ukraine is eligible only for GSP. Through the GSP, the EU is unilaterally decreasing duties on more than 6,000 products that the partner country exports to the EU. This means that the partner country can export its products to the EU on lower tariffs than the MFN would allow. Ukraine is an important beneficiary of the GSP, utilizing 72.2% of the provisions that it is eligible for and an even bigger proportion of it in earlier years. (Dabrowski & Taran, 2012; European Commission, 2013a, 2013b, 2013c) Even though both the MFN and the GSP are important in enhancing trade between Ukraine and the EU, they have serious limitations. They all are just decreasing tariffs, they do not significantly address non-tariff barriers; in other words, they are not instruments of deep integration. Hence, they cannot enhance regulatory or institutional approximation between Ukraine and the EU.

Ukraine and the EU started negotiations on an Association Agreement in 2007. Since then, the EU has changed the framework of its cooperation with its Eastern neighbors and created the Eastern Partnership Agreement. The AA negotiations have been carried on within this framework with the modification that a Deep and Comprehensive Free Trade Agreement (DCFTA) will be attached to it as well. The AA was initialed on 30 March 2012, the DCFTA on 19 July 2012. (European External Action Service, 2013) However, the EU member states are not willing to ratify these agreements yet because of the shortcomings in Ukraine's democratization process. The DCFTA contains widespread trade-related regulatory provisions that will be aiming at overcoming border and behind-the-border trade barriers.[2] The former include the elimination of trade duties and non-tariff-barriers such as import and export restrictions, anti-dumping and anti-subsidy instruments, customs-related requirements and formalities. The latter include measures which will be aiming to change domestic economic institutions that can impede trade flows to and from Ukraine. These include technical regulations as well as technical, sanitary and phytosanitary standards. Moreover, the DCFTA also aims to liberalize trade in services, which requires even further regulatory approximation because it includes several complex sectors. (European Commission, 2013d) All in all, the DCFTA contains several measures that require Ukraine to adopt trade-related aspects of the EU acquis. Hence, it can serve the closer cooperation and integration between the EU and Ukraine.

Western Balkans

The countries of the Western Balkans are interesting for understanding the EU's effect on the countries with which it has trade relations, because these are the countries with the strongest chances of accession. This gives a completely different background for the trade cooperation between the EU and the Western Balkans. Moreover, in the case of the countries of the Western Balkans, the EU is clearly the sole most important trading partner. (Figure 3) This has not changed in most of the countries over the last decade including the

---

2   The DCFTA is not in force at the time of writing this analysis.

years after the global financial crisis.[3] (European Commission Directorate-General for Trade, 2013c, 2013d, 2013e, 2013f, 2013g; International Monetary Fund, 2013; Sanjay, 2008) Nevertheless, there have been changes in the case of a few countries. Albania, for instance, has seen its exports to the EU decrease considerably since 2006 though it is still over 70%. In the case of the Former Yugoslav Republic of Macedonia (FYR Macedonia), the EU's share in its exports has also declined by around 10 percentage points since 2010.[4] Regarding imports, the EU's share decreased by 10-20 percentage points in Albania, Bosnia-Herzegovina and FYR Macedonia during the 2000s, in part owing to these countries taking advantage of East Asian imports. Nevertheless, this trend stabilized in the second half of the 2000s and was even reversed in FYR Macedonia after 2010.

Western Balkan countries have, on the other hand, a weak overall trade performance, resulting in a relatively low volume of trade with the EU. Moreover, the trade structure is also rather unfavorable. As Botrić argues, "the share of intra-industry trade is also relatively low, and the structure of products traded is relatively unfavorable and not improving. The simple continuance of current trends would most likely lead to nominal stagnation, and real divergence from the main European trading routes. In order to integrate these countries in the common European market in the future, a significant adjustment should take place." (Botrić, 2012, p. 24)

Figure 3. The EU's share in the Western Balkan countries' foreign trade: long-term trends

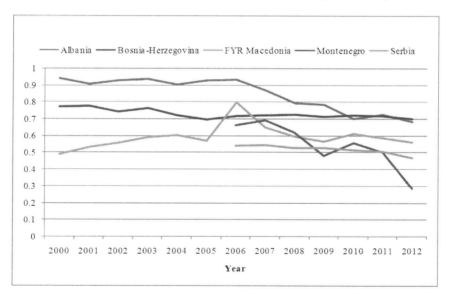

---

3   As Serbia and Montenegro separated in 2006, data is available only from that point on.
4   The sudden decline in 2012 of the EU's share in Montenegro's exports is not confirmed by other sources, so it is assumed to result from measurement problems.

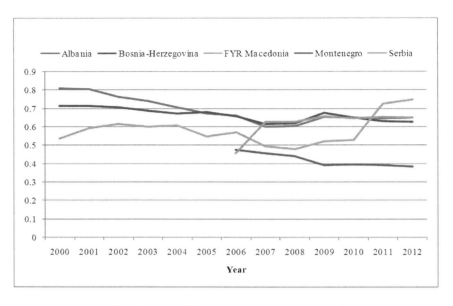

Source: International Monetary Fund, 2013; own calculations.

The relationship between the EU and the Western Balkan countries is guided by the Stabilization and Association Process, within which the EU concluded Stabilization and Association Agreements (SAA) with each individual country between 2001 and 2008. These agreements include a clear association promise and the framework within which the countries can reach it, as well as provisions on the trade connections between the EU and the countries. The aim is to gradually establish a free trade area. (*Integration of the Western Balkans in the EU Internal Market*, 2004)

On the other hand, the EU has had a regional approach in its relations with the Western Balkans since 1996. In order to overcome the historical problems in the region, the EU aimed to promote regional cooperation using trade liberalization as one of the principal instruments. This included not only the Western Balkan countries but the whole South Eastern European region. (Uvalic, 2006) A Memorandum of Understanding on Trade Liberalisation and Facilitation was signed on 27 June 2001 in Brussels, which included the provisions for establishing FTAs among the region's countries in the future. (Pact Working Group on Trade Liberalisation and Facilitation, 2001) Based on this, more than 20 FTAs were concluded in the regions. However, as this approach has been "criticized as representing a 'spaghetti bowl' of differentiated trade relations, creating risks of trade diversion and trade deflection, another important agreement has been concluded among the SEE countries in April 2006 in Bucharest – the Bucharest Declaration. In the 2006 Bucharest Declaration, the SEE countries have committed themselves to transform these FTAs into a single FTA, by means of enlarging and modernizing the current CEFTA [Central European Free Trade Agreement] agreement." (Uvalic, 2006, p. 172)

To summarize, the EU is shaping the trade relations of the Western Balkan countries in two ways. First, through the SAAs it regulates its own relation with these countries individually. The SAAs all include provisions for building free trade regimes between the EU and these countries to facilitate their acquisition of membership. Second, the EU had a vital role in facilitating the emergence of the CEFTA, which aims to liberalize trade among the region's countries. Even though the geographical scope of the two approaches is different, they both represent measures facilitating deep integration, meaning "explicit government action to reduce the market-segmenting effect of domestic policies and regulation, other than tariffs and nontariff barriers." (Sanjay, 2008, p. 69) The overall goal of both measures was to create a single economic space. In the case of the SAAs it is achieved through the direct alignment of the legal and regulatory frameworks with that of the EU. The CEFTA does not stipulate the adoption of the acquis *per se*, but it aims at reducing trade barriers that are higher and more dispersed in the Western Balkans than in the EU. As a result, it is expected to reduce trade diversion and distortions, reduce business transaction costs and administrative strains on customs. (Sanjay, 2008) In practice, this means that the trade regulations in the Western Balkans are getting closer to that of the EU. Indirectly, through the CEFTA, the Western Balkan countries' institutional system is therefore becoming more similar to that of the EU.

Moreover, the EU granted autonomous trade preferences to the Western Balkans in 2000, which were renewed in 2010. These are unilateral preferences, meaning that the EU allows a large range of products from the Western Balkans in its markets without protective measures, such as customs duties, tariff quotas and quantitative restrictions, but does not expect reciprocal measures from these countries. Nevertheless, the protective measures for certain fishery and agricultural products, for instance baby beef, are still enforced. (European Commission, 2013e; Europa.eu, 2009; Europa.eu, 2010) Although these provisions could play an important role in the trade flows between the Western Balkans and the EU, they are not significant for promoting integration between the two regions, because they do not require any institutional changes from the partner countries.

Discussion

The following section aims to give an overview of the changes in the trade relations between the EU and its neighbors based on the case studies above. The case studies have discussed larger trends than those related to the global crisis. However, in this section I follow on the period since the global crisis and try to draw conclusions on its consequences despite the limited time frame. As described at the beginning of the chapter, I divided the problem laid out in the research project into two questions.

The first is whether trade relations between the EU and its neighbors have become weaker since the global crisis. The overall project starts from the assumption that the EU's economic power has considerably weakened since the crisis. However, as this chapter concentrates on trade issues, it is necessary to first examine whether this was indeed the case, or more precisely, whether the consequences of losing economic power can be detected in the EU's trade relations with its neighbors. Regarding this question, all three cases show a rather similar picture, whether analyzing quantitative or qualitative indicators: in none of the three cases can we see a diversion from tendencies before the 2007-2009 crisis. This means that even when data shows that trade ties have weakened, that development is not new but is in line with earlier tendencies. Whether we can see a trend change is important in order to separate the effect of the 2007 – 2009 crisis. A shift in the EU's share after 2007 or 2008, compared to the earlier situation, could be a sign that the crisis fundamentally affected the trade relations between the EU and its partners. It is possible to reach such a clear conclusion because no other shock comparable to the global crisis happened at the same time that could have fundamentally affected these trade relations. However, no significant change in the trend implies that the global crisis did not affect the trade relations considerably.

The individual cases show the following picture. First, I analyzed quantitative measures, namely the share of the EU in its neighbors' exports and imports. Turkey's exports and imports followed very divergent paths. Exports to the EU showed a sudden 8 percentage point drop from 2007 to 2008, after which they stabilized for a few years before decreasing again at a similar pace after 2011. As for the imports, there has been a constant decrease in the EU's share since 2003, which stopped temporarily in 2008 but continued afterwards. Hence, it can be concluded that in the case of Turkey, the global crisis temporarily halted the decline of the EU's trade power, which had started already before (mostly for imports). In other words, based on the trade shares, it can be argued that the EU's economic power in Turkey has decreased, though not as a result of the global crisis: interestingly, the crisis stopped this tendency for a short period.

Exports and imports developed differently in Ukraine as well. The share of the EU in the exports decreased constantly after 2003, altogether by 15 percentage point by 2009, after which the tendency was reversed and a slight increase started. For imports, the share of the EU increased until 2007, when it was reversed and declined by 5.5 percentage points within five years. Thus, in the case of Ukraine, the effect of the global crisis is ambiguous. Export trends show that the EU's trade power has increased concomitantly with the global crisis, which is rather counterintuitive. As regards imports, the trade power of the EU started to decline due to a trend change in 2007. Whether this happened due to the global crisis is highly questionable. The liquidity crisis in Europe started already in 2007. However, we cannot automatically conclude that this translated immediately into the trade relations, not only because this was just the start of the crisis, so the macroeconomic consequences were still limited, but also because of Ukraine's other ongoing domestic problems.

Similarly to the above two, the Western Balkan countries also show a different picture regarding their exports and imports. The EU's share of exports had been declining since 2006 – 2007 to different extents in all the countries except Bosnia-Herzegovina. However, similar to Turkey, this trend was temporarily reversed in some of them around 2009. In Bosnia-Herzegovina, the share of the EU in the exports has been stable. Regarding the imports, a trend change can be detected in 2008 – 2009 in all countries. However, this is rather counterintuitive as in all of them the earlier decline of the EU's share stopped. In Bosnia-Herzegovina a slight decline started again after a temporary increase in the EU's share; in Albania, Montenegro and Serbia it stagnated. The most surprising is the situation of FYR Macedonia, where after 2008 the EU's share in the imports started to increase at an increasingly faster pace. Based on this, there is no evidence that the EU's trade power declined in the Western Balkans due to the global crisis. There had been an erosion of the EU's trade power but this was reversed temporarily or in some cases even permanently concomitantly with the global crisis. All in all, based on the quantitative indicators examined (the EU's share in the analyzed countries' exports and imports), there is no evidence that the EU's trade power has declined due to the global crisis. In most cases the EU is losing its relative position in the trade profile of these countries, but this trend started before the global crisis and was not related to it. Moreover, in some cases it seems that the crisis has even strengthened the EU's position, though no causal link can be established on that point.

In order to establish whether the EU's trade power has declined, it is important to analyze qualitative measures as well, meaning the depth of the trade agreement between the EU and its neighboring countries. In this regard, there have been no significant changes during the global crisis. Trade relations between the EU and Turkey have been regulated by the same agreement since 1996. Ukraine has been negotiating over a deeper agreement since 2007; this was not stopped or considerably slowed down due to the global crisis. SAAs were concluded with all Western Balkan countries even during the global crisis but no significant changes have happened since then. All in all, based on the qualitative indicators, there again is no evidence that the EU has considerably lost trade power in the neighboring countries.

I now turn to the second question, namely whether trade relations between the EU and the neighboring countries are such as to considerably help integration with the EU. This can clearly be separated from the first question. Even though there is no evidence of a significant decline in the EU's trade power in the neighboring countries during the global crisis, this does not mean that these trade relations can play a role in the integration of these countries. Moreover, it is well known that the economic power of the EU in general has declined, even though it is not detectable in the trade relations. Hence, it is important to analyze whether the trade aspect can compensate for other problems the EU might face in asserting its waning economic power. In order to analyze this aspect, one needs to examine the extent of the EU's ability to influence institutions and regulations in the partner countries through the trade agreements it signs with them. As described earlier, this is closely related to the depth of the integration established by these regulations. In the following I summarize the findings for each case study in turn.

The Customs Union between the EU and Turkey is a deep and complex regime whose conclusion meant a large degree of institutional alignment. (Evans et al., 2004) In order to create a common external trade border with the EU, Turkey needed to adopt regulation in several areas that affect parts of its economic system not directly related to trade issues, for instance competition policy. However, this was a one-time change that has not continued since. This means that even though several institutions were integrated between Turkey and the EU, there has been no further change in the last 20 years. As this agreement is long-standing, its influence can be considered well-institutionalized by now. This also implies that its consequences for the integration of Turkey have already been played out. As described in the case study analyzing Turkey's trade relation with the EU, the Customs Union agreement also has several negative consequences for Turkey because of its asymmetric nature. All this makes the integration factor of the EU-Turkey trade agreement rather limited.

Moreover, as described earlier, Turkey's relations with the EU have been undermined by several political problems surrounding Turkey's membership aspirations. The prospects opened by the trade agreement are not strong enough to overcome these in a context in which Turkey's understanding of its own economic role is changing and it is aiming to become a leader instead of a follower. All in all, I see limited possibility for Turkey's integration with the EU through trade relations in light of other issues surrounding the relations.

Trade relations between Ukraine and the EU show an even clearer picture. The Partnership and Cooperation Agreement currently in place does not contain elements promoting deep integration. This means that its possible consequences for Ukraine's integration with the EU are highly limited. However, the implementation of the DCFTA related to the AA can fundamentally change the situation. In the form it was signed in 2012, it contains several promising aspects regarding possible institutional changes that can serve the integration of Ukraine with the EU. Naturally, the future of this agreement will depend to a large extent on the outcome of the political situation that emerged after then-President Yanukovich left the country in February 2014.

Finally, regarding trade agreement between the EU and the Western Balkan countries, it can be argued that, of the three cases studied, the Western Balkan countries are those whose integration prospects are best served by the trade agreements with the EU. The SAAs have very clear integration goals and are designed to prepare the accession of these countries to the EU. Hence, they are clear examples of trade integration measures. Moreover, it is also important to note that the EU has a considerably different trade weight in these countries than in the other two cases. It is still responsible for more than 50% of most countries' exports and imports. This gives it much more power to influence these countries' domestic issues based purely on the trade relations. Nevertheless, as part of its new foreign policy, Turkey has started to build up capabilities in the Western Balkans. (Szigetvári, 2012) Even though Turkey's position is still weak at the moment compared to the EU, a well-managed relationship there would lead to a considerable repositioning in the EU's neighborhood.

Conclusion

The main goal of this chapter was to analyze the trade relations between the EU and its neighboring countries as well as how these affect the power of the EU in these countries. I aimed to separate the influence of trade connections from other sectors where the EU cooperates with these countries. In order to do so, I analyzed the EU's share in the partner countries' exports and imports as well as the trade agreements and their consequences for institutional transfer and integration, concentrating on changes that happened since the global crisis. The cases analyzed were Ukraine, Turkey and the Western Balkans.

Fundamental changes were expected only in the quantitative variables, not in the qualitative ones, as starting or changing trade agreements require longer time frames than the seven years that have elapsed since the start of the crisis. However, the analysis of the individual cases showed no fundamental changes in the EU's share in any of the partner countries' exports or imports. This implies that the EU's trade power has not changed significantly since the start of the global crisis. However, the limited time period that has elapsed makes it difficult to draw clear conclusions over its future trajectory. Similarly, the examination of the trade agreements showed no fundamental changes since the start of the global crisis. All in all, the EU's trade relations did not change trajectory since the start of the crisis.

Even though the three cases present no major differences in their respective changes since the start of the crisis, the picture presented by the current state of affairs is different. The EU's share in the exports and imports of these countries shows high diversity. The lowest is in Ukraine with 20 – 25% for the exports and around 30% for the imports. In Turkey, the EU's share is a bit below 40% for both sectors. The EU's share in the trade volume is the highest in the Western Balkan countries with considerable differences among the individual countries: the share in exports ranges between 47% and 70%, and between 39% and 75% for imports. The state of the trade agreements reflects the same picture. The PCA in force with Ukraine does little to serve deep integration between Ukraine and the EU. The

SAAs with the Western Balkan countries go considerably deeper, but it is the Customs Union governing the trade relations between the EU and Turkey that is the most supportive of institutional transfer.

To summarize, the analysis found that the global crisis did not cause major changes in the development of the trade relations between the EU and its neighboring countries. On the other hand, the *status quo* that started to take form has resulted in considerable diversity in the region. Ukraine is clearly the least tied to the EU, while Turkey and the Western Balkan countries' relative ranking depends on whether quantitative or the qualitative indicators are used.

The above summarized the findings of the chapter based on its narrow agenda, namely examining trade relations separately of other aspects of the cooperation between the EU and these countries and strictly concentrating on the period since the global crisis. However, these results have rather limited validity for future trends. On the one hand the examined time period is short, which restricts the possible conclusions that can be drawn. On the other hand, completely separating trade issues from other aspects of the integration is not only difficult but also rather controversial. Negotiations leading to a trade agreement are always highly political; hence, the relations between the partners on other issues will influence them. Moreover, in most cases the trade agreements were part of a larger framework of cooperation between the EU and the partner countries, most clearly with the Western Balkans, where the trade agreement is only part of the SAA, and with Ukraine, where the new DCFTA would be part of the political AA agreement. Hence, in order to draw sensible policy conclusions, the larger situation needs to be examined.

Based on the larger trends of trade relations and stepping out of the narrow agenda of this chapter, the picture regarding the trade power of the EU is not entirely positive. While the Customs Union with Turkey did bring considerable institutional alignment when it was implemented, there has been no further progress since 1996. The implementation of the DCFTA was stopped due to domestic issues in Ukraine. The SAA are more forward-looking but they can only have an effect if their agenda is fully implemented. All this means that in order to maintain the integration with these countries, the EU needs to take clear and credible steps towards them. On trade issues, for instance, this means a clear commitment to integrating these countries with the EU's trade in such a way as to enable them to influence their own fate. This would be important in order to avoid the problem of Turkey, which is in a highly asymmetric relationship due to the arrangements in the Customs Union agreement. The cooperation needs to go further than the removal of border protection measures and needs to include measures to align regulation and production processes as well. Even though these are not directly related to trade, as argued earlier, they are inevitable for true trade integration. Moreover, the EU needs to realize that during the last decade or so, it ceased to be the only or dominant trading partner in its neighborhood. Turkey's status is changing from being a clear trade partner to being a competitor of the EU in the Western Balkans. Moreover, countries from other regions are also gaining importance. In order to change these developments, the EU may need to rethink its trade agenda with these countries and to develop strategies that fit the partner countries' current foreign policies and level of economic development. However, reaching these goals will probably only be possible through a combination of trade integration and integration in other sectors.

Bibliography

Akçalı, E. (2013). Untitled Address on "EU-Turkey Relations in 2013: Increasing Momentum and Facing Regional Challenges" [Panel]. Center for EU Enlargement Studies, Central European University, 25.09.2013.

Akgün, M. (2013). Untitled Address on "EU-Turkey Relations in 2013: Increasing Momentum and Facing Regional Challenges" [Panel]. Center for EU Enlargement Studies, Central European University, 25.09.2013.

Babacan, M. (2011). Whither an Axis Shift: A Perspective from Turkey's Foreign Trade. *Insight Turkey*. 13(1), 129–157. Retrieved from http://file.insightturkey.com/Files/Pdf/insight-turkey_vol_13_no_1_2011_babacan.pdf Visited: 11.09.2013.

Botrić, V. (2012). Intra-industry Trade between the European Union and Western Balkans: A Close-up. (EIZ Working Papers EIZ-WP-1202). Zagreb: Ekonomski Institut Zagreb.

Dabrowski, M., & Taran, S. (2012). The Free Trade Agreement between the EU and Ukraine: Conceptual Background, Economic Context and Potential Impact. (CASE Network Studies & Analyses No. 437/2012). Warsaw: CASE - Center for Social and Economic Research. Retrieved from http://www.case-research.eu/sites/default/files/publications/CNSA_2012_437.pdf Visited: 11.09.2013

Europa.eu. (2009). Exceptional trade measures 2000-2009. Retrieved from http://europa.eu/legislation_summaries/enlargement/western_balkans/r18000_en.htm. Visited 9.09.2013.

Europa.eu. (2010) Exceptional trade measures 2010. Retrieved from http://europa.eu/legislation_summaries/enlargement/western_balkans/el0004_en.htm. Visited 9.09.2013.

European Commission. (2013a). Ukraine - Trade. Retrieved from http://ec.europa.eu/trade/policy/countries-and-regions/countries/ukraine/. Visited 15.09.2013.

European Commission. (2013b). Generalised Scheme of Preferences (GSP) - Trade. Retrieved from http://ec.europa.eu/trade/policy/countries-and-regions/development/generalised-scheme-of-preferences/. Visited 15.09.2013.

European Commission. (2013c). The EU's new Generalised Scheme of Preferences (GSP). Trade. Retrieved from http://trade.ec.europa.eu/doclib/docs/2012/december/tradoc_150164.pdf. Visited 15.09.2013.

European Commission. (2013d). EU-Ukraine Deep and Comprehensive Free Trade Area. Retrieved from http://trade.ec.europa.eu/doclib/docs/2013/april/tradoc_150981.pdf. Visited 15.09.2013.

European Commission. (2013e). Western Balkans - Trade. Retrieved from http://ec.europa.eu/trade/policy/countries-and-regions/regions/western-balkans/. Visited 15.09.2013.

European Commission Directorate-General for Trade. (2013a). Turkey, EU Bilateral Trade and Trade with the World. DG Trade Statistics. Retrieved from http://trade.ec.europa.eu/doclib/docs/2006/september/tradoc_113456.pdf. Visited 9.09.2013.

European Commission Directorate-General for Trade. (2013b). Ukraine, EU Bilateral Trade and Trade with the World. DG Trade Statistics. Retrieved from http://trade.ec.europa.eu/doclib/docs/2006/september/tradoc_113459.pdf. Visited 9.09.2013.

European Commission Directorate-General for Trade. (2013c). Albania, EU Bilateral Trade and Trade with the World. DG Trade Statistics. Retrieved from http://trade.ec.europa.eu/doclib/docs/2006/september/tradoc_113342.pdf. Visited 9.09.2013.

European Commission Directorate-General for Trade. (2013d). FYR Macedonia, EU Bilateral Trade and Trade with the World. DG Trade Statistics. Retrieved from http://trade. ec.europa.eu/doclib/docs/2006/september/tradoc_113381.pdf. Visited 9.09.2013.

European Commission Directorate-General for Trade. (2013e). Montenegro, EU Bilateral Trade and Trade with the World. DG Trade Statistics. Retrieved from http://trade. ec.europa.eu/doclib/docs/2008/august/tradoc_140030.pdf. Visited 9.09.2013.

European Commission Directorate-General for Trade. (2013f). Serbia, EU Bilateral Trade and Trade with the World. DG Trade Statistics. Retrieved from http://trade.ec.europa. eu/doclib/docs/2008/august/tradoc_140028.pdf. Visited 9.09.2013.

European Commission Directorate-General for Trade. (2013g). Bosnia-Herzegovina, EU Bilateral Trade and Trade with the World. DG Trade Statistics. Retrieved from http:// trade.ec.europa.eu/doclib/docs/2006/september/tradoc_113358.pdf. Visited 9.09.2013.

European External Action Service. (2013). Information on the EU-Ukraine Association Agreement. Retrieved from http://eeas.europa.eu/top_stories/2012/140912_ ukraine_en.htm. Visited 5.08.2013.

Evans, D., Holmes, P., Iacovone, L., & Robinson, S. (2004). *A Framework for Evaluating Regional Trade Agreements: Deep Integration and New Regionalism.* University of Sussex. Retrieved from http://www.sussex.ac.uk/Units/PRU/tradelib_firms_Robinson.pdf Visited: 21.08.2013.

Integration of the Western Balkans in the EU Internal Market (2004) Retrieved from http://www. westernbalkans.info/htmls/save_pdf2.php?id=550 Visited 9.9.2013.

Lawrence, R. Z. (1996). *Regionalism, Multilateralism, and Deeper Integration Integrating National Economies.* Washington, DC: Brookings Institution Press.

McNamara, S., Cohen, A., & Phillips, J. (2010). Countering Turkey's Strategic Drift. (Backgrounder No. 2442). Washington, DC: The Heritage Foundation. Retrieved from http://thf_media.s3.amazonaws.com/2010/pdf/bg2442.pdf Visited: 26.7.2013.

N. Rózsa, E. (2013). Untitled Address on "EU-Turkey Relations in 2013: Increasing Momentum and Facing Regional Challenges" [Panel]. Center for EU Enlargement Studies, Central European University, 25.09.2013.

Partnership and Cooperation Agreement between the European Communities and their Member States, and Ukraine (1998). Official Journal of the European Communities L49. Retrieved from http://ec.europa.eu/world/agreements/downloadFile.do?fullText=yes&treatyTrans Id=659 Visited: 12.9.2013.

Sanjay, K. (Ed., 2008). *Western Balkan Integration and the EU. An Agenda for Trade and Growth.* Washington, DC: The International Bank for Reconstruction and Development/The World Bank. Retrieved from http://siteresources.worldbank.org/ECAEXT/Resources/publications/454763-1213051861605/9780821374726.pdf Visited: 3.9.2013.

Stability Pact Working Group on Trade Liberalisation and Facilitation. (2001). Memorandum of Understanding on Trade Liberalisation and Facilitation, Brussels, 27 June 2001. Retrieved from http://www.stabilitypact.org/trade/Memorandum of Understanding on Trade Liberalisation and Facilitation.pdf. Visited 15.09.2013.

Szigetvári, T. (2012). Turkey is back - Turkish interest on the Western Balkans. (EU Frontiers Study No. 9). Budapest: Center for EU Enlargement Studies. Retrieved from https:// cens.ceu.hu/sites/default/files/publications/policypaperno9eufrontierstamas-szigetvari.pdf Visited: 25.8.2013.

Szigetvári, T. (2013a). Törökország gazdasági átalakulása és külgazdasági expanziója. *Külügyi Szemle*. 12(1), 22–38.

Szigetvári, T. (2013b). Untitled Address on "EU-Turkey Relations in 2013: Increasing Momentum and Facing Regional Challenges" [Panel]. Budapest: Center for EU Enlargement Studies, Central European University, 25.09.2013.

Tófalvi, F. (2014). The forever candidate – Turkey and the EU. In P. Balázs, *Europe's Position in the New World Order* (pp. 157-182). Budapest: CEU Press.

Turkish Statistical Institute. (2013). *Foreign Trade Statistics Database*. Retrieved from http://tuikapp.tuik.gov.tr/disticaretapp/menu_ing.zul. Visited 14.09.2013.

Ülgen, S., & Zahariadis, Y. (2004). The Future of Turkish-EU Trade Relations - Deepening vs Widening. *Turkish Policy Quarterly*. 3(4). Retrieved from http://www.turkishpolicy.com/dosyalar/files/TPQ2004-4-ulgen.pdf Visited: 25.8.2013.

Uvalic, M. (2006). Trade in Southeast Europe: recent trends and some policy implications. *The European Journal of Comparative Economics*. 3(2), 171–195.

World Trade Organisation Trade Policy Review Body. (2012). Trade policy review - Report by the Secreteriat - Turkey. Retrieved from http://www.wto.org/english/tratop_e/tpr_e/tp359_e.htm Visited 9.09.2013.

POSSIBILITIES OF SECURITY AND DEFENSE COOPERATION BETWEEN THE EUROPEAN UNION AND UKRAINE

ANDRÁS RÁCZ[1]

The aim of this chapter is to study the possibilities for security and defense cooperation between the European Union (EU) and Ukraine. Taking into account the well-researched military capability shortages of the EU's Common Security and Defense Policy (CSDP) of the European Union, the chapter focuses on those fields where Ukraine can meaningfully contribute to bridging these capability gaps.

The main research question is therefore the following: in which security and defense policy fields can Ukraine contribute to the crisis management activities of the Common Security and Defense Policy? Connected to this, the chapter also examines how closer EU-Ukraine cooperation in the CSDP could be beneficial for the Visegrad countries.

The chapter is composed of five main parts. The introduction is followed by an overview of Ukraine's remarkable contributions to international crisis management operations. Second, Ukraine's contribution to the CSDP is discussed, both in terms of the legal background and of the experience accumulated so far. The third chapter focuses on Ukraine's strategic airlift capabilities, which have long attracted the attention of both the North Atlantic Treaty Organization (NATO) and the EU, while the fourth chapter provides the reader with an overview of the possibilities for cooperation in the defense industry. The chapter ends with a fifth, concluding chapter. It is important to note that the background research for this chapter was conducted before the start in November 2013 of the crisis in Ukraine. Hence, it does not reflect on the political changes that have taken place since then.

Ukraine: a remarkable contributor to international crisis management operations

Ukraine is, by virtue of its constitution, a neutral country. The country's non-aligned, non-block status is set out in both the 1991 Declaration of Independence and the 1996 constitution. (Potapkina, 2010) The National Security Strategy, last amended in 2012, keeps to this commitment and confirms the need for a non-aligned security policy.[2] The Strategic Defence Bulletin of 2012 also follows this policy line.[3]

---

1   The views presented are the author's own and in no way represent the official position of either the Central European University or the Finnish Institute of International Affairs.
2   See http://zakon1.rada.gov.ua/laws/show/389/2012/paran5#n5, Article 4.2.6.
3   See http://www.president.gov.ua/documents/14824.html

However, this policy of non-alignment does not prevent Ukraine from closely cooperating with various international security organizations, including both NATO and the Collective Security Treaty Organization (CSTO), in addition to the United Nations (UN), the Commonwealth of Independent States (CIS) and the Organization for Security and Co-operation in Europe (OSCE). The Strategic Defence Bulletin also confirms the need for an increased participation in international crisis management operations as well.[4]

Ukraine has a long record of participating in various international crisis management operations, ranging from UN and OSCE missions to EU and NATO-led ones. (For a detailed map of Ukrainian participation in international peacekeeping missions, see Ministry of Defence of Ukraine, 2014, p. 57) According to the UN Department of Peacekeeping Operations (UNDPKO), Ukraine has been a remarkable contributor to UN operations over the last fifteen years.

Figure 1. Ukraine's participation in UN peacekeeping operations
Source: United Nations (Undated).

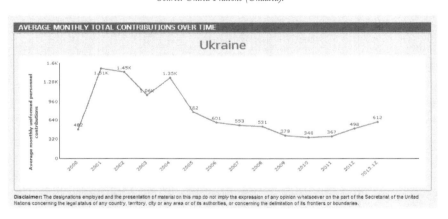

This high level of participation means that Ukrainian armed forces have accumulated considerable experience and knowledge on operating in international crisis management operations. In the first half of the 2000s, Ukraine was the topmost European contributor to UN-led operations. As of December 2013 Ukraine, with its 612 personnel, holds the third place in Europe, following Italy (1,118 personnel) and France (952). The largest UN operation Ukraine is participating in is the UNMIL in Liberia, with 279 personnel. Besides troop contributions, special Ukrainian aviation detachments are serving in Liberia and in the UNOCI in the Ivory Coast, operating both Mi-8 transport and Mi-24 attack helicopters.[5]

As the non-aligned status does not prevent intensive cooperation, Ukraine has also been actively working together with NATO. Ukraine was the first CIS country to sign the Partnership for Peace Framework document in 1994, and in 1997 the NATO Ukraine

---

4   Ibid.
5   http://www.mil.gov.ua/diyalnist/mirotvorchist/uchast-zbrojnih-sil-ukraini-u-mizhnarodnih-operacziyah-z-pidtrimannya-miru-i-bezpeki.html

Special Partnership Charter was signed as well. A NATO Liaison Office has been operating in Kyiv since 1999.

Currently the most important areas of NATO-Ukraine cooperation are the ongoing reform of the military, including the creation of a more effective defense planning system, training support, improved democratic control of the armed forces, etc.

The long-term objective is to improve the interoperability of the Ukrainian armed forces with NATO. The already mentioned Strategic Defence Bulletin confirms the need to improve interoperability with "the respective units of multilateral formations."[6]

Though NATO is not specifically mentioned, the document states:

Ukraine will continue activities to achieve the required level of interoperability of the designated units of the Defence Forces by introducing certain criteria and standards in the area of Defence Planning, training support of specific military authorities and units for joint activity with the armed forces of international security organizations.[7]

As these points are exactly in line with the current priorities of NATO-Ukraine cooperation, and although NATO is not mentioned by name, the orientation of the defense reform is quite clear. In other words, Ukraine's non-aligned status helped in many respects to intensify its cooperation with NATO. (Alexandrov, 2012, p. 35) All in all, Ukraine seems to be building an armed force which ambitions to become NATO-compatible, though without ambitioning NATO accession.

In line with this commitment, Ukraine has been an active participant in of NATO's ongoing crisis management operations. (Lorenz, 2013) Ukrainian soldiers serve in Afghanistan and in the NATO Training Mission in Iraq, more than 130 Ukrainian servicemen are working in the KFOR in Kosovo, and a Ukrainian warship is taking part in NATO's Operation Active Endeavour in the Mediterranean.[8]

Ukraine-EU crisis management cooperation

Ukraine's rich experience in international crisis management operations, discussed above, means Kyiv clearly has the potential to become a valuable partner of the EU as well. However, so far the Ukrainian participation in EU missions has been rather limited.

The Eastern enlargement of the European Union in 2004 fundamentally changed the nature of the challenges facing the EU's foreign, security and defense policy. Enlargement brought several regional conflicts closer to the borders of the EU, such as the Moldova-Transnistria issue, the multi-layered crises of the Balkans, or, in a broader context, the instability of the Sub-Saharan region. (For a good summary, see Missiroli, 2003)

Already the Wider Europe framework put forward in 2003 reflected the increased importance of regional crises, and stressed the need for more intensive European participation in resolving them. (Commission of the European Communities, 2003, p. 12) The document called for a more active policy presence in the crisis regions, not only to ac-

---

6   http://www.president.gov.ua/documents/14824.html

7   Ibid.

8   http://www.mil.gov.ua/diyalnist/mirotvorchist/uchast-zbrojnih-sil-ukraini-u-mizhnarodnih-operacziyah-z-pidtrimannya-miru-i-bezpeki.html

tively increase the chances of a resolution, but also to demonstrate the EU's commitment to regional stability.

The European Neighbourhood Policy (ENP) Strategy Paper, launched in 2004 together with the country-specific Country Reports, used an already much more concrete wording, regarding cooperation in terms of conflict prevention and crisis management. (Commission of the European Communities, 2004) The Country Report on Ukraine concretely mentioned Ukraine's "possible participation in EU-led crisis management operations," in addition to crisis management, exchange of information and joint training. (Ibid., p. 13)

Kyiv was open for an agreement on closer crisis management cooperation with the EU, particularly in the light of the Moldova-Transnistria conflict that directly affected Ukraine. The "Agreement between the European Union and Ukraine establishing a framework for the participation of Ukraine in the European Union crisis management operations," originally to be adopted in the autumn of 2004, was finally signed only in June 2005 owing to the "Orange Revolution." (Official Journal of the European Union, 2005a) One should also mention the Agreement between Ukraine and the European Union on the security procedures for the exchange of classified information, also signed in June 2005, which enabled the necessary information exchange between the EU and Ukraine. (Official Journal of the European Union, 2005b) The ratification of the two agreements was nonetheless delayed until March 2008 and December 2006 respectively, owing to domestic political reasons. (Mission of Ukraine to the European Union, 2012)

However, despite the delay in the ratification, the agreement created the background for Ukraine to participate in the EUPM Police Mission in Bosnia-Herzegovina from 2006 until its end in 2012. (Ibid.) Ukraine is also contributing to the anti-piracy operation EUNAVFOR ATALANTA. Since 2010 a Ukrainian staff officer has been serving at the Northwood Headquarters of the Mission, and since March 2013 the frigate Hetman Sahaydachnyi is participating in the operation as well.[9]

Though this bears no direct relationship with the two documents mentioned above, the European Union Border Assistance Mission to Moldova (EUBAM), launched in December 2005, fits well into the political context of these agreements. The EUBAM operates in part from Ukrainian soil (its headquarters are located in Odessa), with, of course, the participation of numerous Ukrainian border guards and civilians.

In line with the current state of the Ukrainian defense reform, Kyiv's interest is mostly directed towards tactical-level cooperation and contribution to the EU-led battle groups. (Bugriy, 2013) In July 2011 Ukraine therefore joined the EU Battle Group HELBROC alongside forces from Greece, Bulgaria, Romania and Cyprus, with a marines company equipped with armored personnel carriers as well as an Il-76 transport aircraft for an original duration of six months. (Worldwide News Ukraine, 2011) This commitment turned out to be a lasting one: from January 2014 Ukrainian units were again on permanent alert and ready to be deployed in the areas of responsibility of the HELBROC (currently named Balkan Battle Group). (Black Sea News, 2014)

The participation of Ukraine in the Balkan Battle Group led to an official proposal that Ukrainian armed forces also work with the Visegrad Battle Group (BG), which is to be established in 2016. Poland will be its host nation, and the battle group will be composed of

---

9   http://www.mil.gov.ua/diyalnist/mirotvorchist/uchast-zbrojnih-sil-ukraini-u-mizhnarodnih-
     operacziyah-z-pidtrimannya-miru-i-bezpeki.html

some 2,500 troops: 950 from Poland, 750 from the Czech Republic, and 400 from Hungary and Slovakia each.

However, the planned Visegrad Battle Group comes with a number of shortcomings that have to be addressed. Rotary wing capability (e.g. helicopters) is still missing, and so too are medical evacuation, Communication and Information Systems (CIS) support, and also logistics. A question mark also hangs over strategic airlift capability as Hungary needs to evaluate the potential contribution to the Visegrad BG of the NATO Heavy Airlift Wing C-17s stationed at its Pápa airport. (Central European Policy Institute, 2013, p. 2)

Cooperation with Ukraine is an obvious choice in order to bridge some of this capability gap. The possible involvement of Ukraine was reportedly already discussed in 2007 at the meeting of the Visegrad chiefs of staff, but was not realized at the time. (Balcer, 2013) However, in April 2013 the Visegrad Group officially invited Ukraine to participate in the Visegrad Battle Group. The issues of cooperation discussed at the April 2013 Sopot meeting included control of airspace, strengthening of cross-border ties, joint military exercises, language training for Ukrainian officers, etc. (Ukrinform, 2013) The Program of the Hungarian Presidency of the Visegrad Cooperation already mentioned the battle group as a V4+Ukraine unit. (Hungarian Presidency of the Visegrad Group, Undated, p.5)

It should however be noted that so far none of the news items published have mentioned anything more concrete on the possible use of Ukrainian military capabilities in the Visegrad Battle Group, despite Ukraine's rich experiences in participating in international crisis management missions. As demonstrated by the UN mission to Liberia, Ukraine is able to deploy a helicopter force abroad, and possesses the much-needed strategic airlift capability. According to *The Military Balance*, the Ukrainian Army possesses more than 130 Mi-24 attack helicopters and 38 Mi-8 transport helicopters, in addition to the Navy's more than 70 anti-submarine warfare helicopters and the Air Force's 34 transport helicopters: these are major helicopter capabilities that the Visegrad Battle Group could rely on. (International Institute for Strategic Studies, 2013, pp. 239-240)

Ukraine's strategic airlift capabilities

One of the most important shortfalls of European defense policy is the absence of strategic airlift capabilities, i.e. the lack of proper heavy transport planes. The core problem is that despite the growing ambitions of the EU's Common Security and Defense Policy, the Union still lacks the strategic airlift capabilities necessary for crisis management in distant regions. (See Karlsson, Undated, p. 18) The problem is well researched in the CSDP literature; one may mention, for example, Gustav Lindström's detailed capabilities analysis, conducted in 2007, or Katia Vlachos-Dengler's study from the same year. (Lindstrom, 2007; Vlachos-Dengler, 2007)

Many among the 28 member states of the EU possess some form of strategic airlift capability, yet with the exception of the United Kingdom they all use obsolete planes with small carrying capacities and short effective ranges. These are either various versions of the C-130 Hercules purchased from the United States, or the C-160 Transall built through French-German cooperation and put into service in the late 1960s. Despite several improvement efforts, most of these planes are simply not adequate given the requirements of rapid reaction and global operational reach.

Table 1. Strategic airlift capabilities of the EU28

Type	Payload [tons]	Maximum troop capacity	Range [km]	Total EU28
A310 MRTT	35	190	8,900	12
C-130 B/E/H	19.3	92	7,800	119
C-130 J	19	128	7,800	50
C-160	16	93	5,100	133
C-17	41	102	8,700	4
TriStar	44	160	9,800	9

Source: Karlsson, Undated, p. 19

Even the most modern versions of the C-130s that are available in relatively high numbers are not able to transport a payload of more than 20 tons. Hence, they are simply not suitable for transporting, for example, the modern infantry fighting vehicles of an EU Battle Group. (Karlsson, Undated) The only exception is the UK, which has been leasing five C-17 heavy airlifters from Boeing since 2009. Additionally only a few of the old TriStars are available. These do not have a proper rear cargo door, rendering them unsuitable for transporting vehicles, and are used mostly for troop transport. (Ibid.)

Moreover the available planes are hardly suitable for the requirements of Petersberg-type missions (short take-off and landing, search and rescue capability, protection against air defense missiles, etc.), either in payload or in operational range. Many of them lack the capabilities necessary for use in a non-permissible environment typical of Petersberg-type missions.

The lack of strategic airlift will not be fully overcome even with the completion of the Airbus 400M planes. With its maximum payload of 37,000 kg the Airbus 400M will not be able to compete with the super-heavy transport planes of the US Air Force, Russia or Ukraine.[10] If such transport capabilities were to become necessary, the EU would still need to rent the required planes from these air forces.

Strategic airlift from Ukraine

As long as the Airbus 400M program is not completed, an important means for the EU to enhance its strategic airlift capabilities on its own – i.e. outside the Berlin Plus agreement, thus without relying on NATO resources – would be to rent the necessary planes either from Russia or from Ukraine. The declared will of enhanced security cooperation in the European Neighbourhood Policy discussed earlier may provide the necessary framework for such an agreement providing access to Ukraine's strategic airlift capabilities.

---

10 These include the Lockheed C-5 Galaxy (118,000 kg), the McDonell-Douglas C-17 (78,000 kg), the Antonov An-124 (150,000 kg), the An-22 (80,000 kg), and the Ilyushin Il-76 (40,000 kg)

Table 2. Ukraine's strategic air transport capabilities (including both military and civilian)

Type	Range [km]	Maximum payload	Cruise speed	Available
Antonov An-72A	4,300	10,000 KG	550 KM/H	26+
Antonov An-124	6,700	150,000 KG	800 KM/H	7
Ilyushin Il-76MD	6,700	48,000 KG	750 KM/H	20
Tupolev Tu-134	3,200	8,200 KG	750 KM/H	2

Source: International Institute for Strategic Studies (2013).

As is clear from Table 2, the Ukrainian Air Force possesses airplanes with significantly greater strategic airlift capacity than any of the EU member states' air forces. The heavy transport planes (An-124 and Il-76) have no equivalents in the air forces of EU member states except for the five leased C-5s of the Royal Air Force. The remarkable number of Il-76 heavy airplanes would in particular offer a pool of strategic airlift resources, even on a permanent basis if necessary.

Both the European Union and NATO started exploring ways of getting access to Ukrainian strategic airlift capabilities in the early 2000s. NATO and Ukraine signed a Memorandum of Understanding (MOU) on Strategic Airlift in June 2004. (NATO, 2004) Based on the positive experience gained from using Ukraine's heavy airplanes, and on the prevailing shortages of strategic airlift, in January 2006 NATO and Ruslan SALIS GmbH signed the agreement on Strategic Airlift Interim Solution (SALIS), which came into force in March of the same year, after Sweden joined as the sixteenth partner country. Ruslan SALIS GmbH is a subsidiary of the Russian-based, German-registered Volga-Dnepr Airlines, which closely cooperates with Ukraine's Antonov Design Bureau and Antonov Airlines. After the original SALIS contract expired, the group won a new contract for the 2012-2014 period, with a possible extension until 2017.

In the framework of this agreement, NATO uses six chartered Antonov An-124-100 super-heavy transport airplanes that are able to transport oversized cargo over a large distance. (See NATO, 2014) These planes fly regular sorties to Afghanistan, participating in supplying the NATO forces there. They have also been used on one-off missions such as during the earthquake in Pakistan in October 2005 or for supporting the African Union's peacekeeping mission in Darfur. (Ibid.) The Pakistani earthquake relief operation was particularly interesting because it took place even before the SALIS agreement was actually signed: the framework used was the 2004 Memorandum of Understanding mentioned above.

The European Union turned its attention towards Ukrainian strategic airlift capabilities after the June 2002 Seville European Council meeting and its resulting agreement on expanded military cooperation with the partner countries. (Kuzio, 2003, p.23) At the Copenhagen EU-Ukraine summit on 4 July 2002, further improvements were reached on the issue of using Ukrainian strategic airlift capabilities for EU military operations. (European Union-Ukraine Summit, 2002, p. 2)

Kyiv was open to an agreement under which the EU would be guaranteed the use of its heavy transport aircrafts in military operations. However, the already mentioned Ukraine - EU Agreement on Ukrainian participation in EU operations in crisis management contains no mention of a possible use of Ukraine's strategic airlift capabilities.

In light of the SALIS agreement, one may ask the question of availability, i.e. whether Ukraine has any additional strategic airlifters than the ones already contracted in the framework of the SALIS. The answer is definitely yes. Russia's Volga-Dnepr Airlines, i.e. SALIS's main contractor, alone has ten An-124s, while Antonov Airlines have an additional seven, which means that not all Ukrainian An-124s are bound to the SALIS. (Flightglobal Insight, 2013, p. 8) Additionally, besides the super-heavy Antonov 124s, the Ukrainian Air Force alone possesses twenty Il-76 heavy airlifters. A number of additional Il-76s are also operated by private civilian airlines (e.g. Yuzmashavia) that could be contracted as well. (Ibid.)

All in all, depending on the outcome of the political changes in Ukraine in 2013-2014, the EU may consider again the option of getting contracted access to Ukrainian strategic airlift capabilities. The potential is indeed there.

Possibilities of military industry cooperation

Ukraine inherited an immense share, approximately 30%, of the former Soviet military in-dustrial complex. Though most of these factories were highly ineffective, the Ukrainian leadership was reluctant to modernize, convert or close them because of the political impor-tance of these companies. When Ukraine reached its independence in 1991, the military-industrial complex represented some 50-60% of its overall industry, and the lives of several million Ukrainians – approximately 40% of the working population! - depended on these jobs. (Strekal, 1994, p. 26) Besides the sheer size and inertia of the military-industrial com-plex, another structural problem was that the main profile of the Ukrainian defense industry was to produce parts and equipments for modern weapon systems, but not whole weapons. (Ibid., p. 29) Moreover, dire economic conditions prevented the supply of Ukrainian armed forces with state-of-the-art Ukrainian-made weapons. Changing these unfavorable starting conditions took almost two decades.

Since the mid-2000s, however, the Ukrainian defense industry has become increasingly present on the world market. Besides maintaining their modernization potential, Ukrainian companies have acquired the capability to produce complete weapon systems as well, particu-larly armored personnel carriers, infantry fighting vehicles, transport airplanes and smaller warships. According to data from the Stockholm International Peace Research Institute, Ukraine ranked as the ninth largest arms exporter in the world in 2008-2012, accounting for 2% of the world's arms deliveries. (SIPRI, 2013) Moreover, unlike in the 1990s when Ukraine sold inherited ex-Soviet armaments on a massive scale, posing a serious proliferation threat, arms sales in 2008-2012 already included considerable amounts of new and refurbished weap-ons. (SIPRI, 2012) Concerning new equipments, Ukraine delivered 270 new BTR-4 infantry fighting vehicles to Iraq, another 100 to Kazakhstan, more than 200 BTR-3s to Thailand, four DSL-5612 landing crafts to Venezuela, and dozens of jet engines to various customers. Regarding modernization, one may mention the 128 refurbished T-72 tanks sold to Ethiopia, and the 30 modernized BTR-70s for Georgia. From many points of view, Ukraine has indeed already become a competitor for the Russian military industry; both countries, for instance, put in bids for the Thai tender which was eventually won by Ukraine. Besides, a number of Ukrainian defense companies are already working jointly with Western partners. The Falarick 105 guided anti-tank missile has, for example, been co-developed by the State Kyiv Design Bureau "Luch" and the Belgian CMI Defence. (CMI, 2010) The new European light rocket, the Italian-assembled Vega, flies with a Ukrainian engine. (NRCU, 2013)

In light of these Ukrainian capacities, it is important to note the high number of ex-Soviet military equipments – particularly tanks, infantry fighting vehicles, armored personnel carriers - still in service in those EU member states that belonged to the former Warsaw Pact. Even in just the four Visegrad countries the numbers are remarkable.

Table 3. Ex-Soviet military equipments still in service in the Visegrad countries and refurbished by Ukrainian companies. The list does not include artillery pieces and missiles

Name	Type	Poland	Czech Republic	Slovakia	Hungary	Altogether
BTR80/80A	AIFV/APC	0	0	0	428	428
BMP-1	AIFV	1,297	139	148	0	1,584
BMP-2	AIFV	0	181	91	0	272
T-72	MBT	541	40	30	30	641
Mi-24/35	ATKH	30	24	15	11	80
Mi-8/17	ATKH/TRN	38	28	15	17	98
Mi-2	light helicopter	58	0	6	0	64
MiG-29	fighter	26	0	20	0	46
SU-22	fighter/attack	26	0	0	0	26

Source: International Institute for Strategic Studies (2013).

The military equipments listed in Table 3 are all either inherited from the Warsaw Pact, or were procured shortly after the fall of the Soviet Union (for example, Hungary's T-72s). Simply due to their age, a growing number of these weapon systems need to be either refurbished or replaced. The exact numbers and the pace of ageing of these equipments are beyond the focus of the current research, but the trend is anyway obvious.

Hence, in light of its already studied capabilities, Ukraine could indeed be an option both for the refurbishment and the replacement of these weapon systems. Concerning the legal aspects, many Ukrainian companies have the producer's license to modernize or modify these ex-Soviet equipments. For example, Motor Sich has a closed-type cycle for overhauling Mi-2, Mi-8/17 and Mi-24/35 helicopters. (Ukrainian Defense Review, 2013a) Thus the main question is more political, i.e. whether any country would consider contracting a Ukrainian company, rather than a Russian one, for military equipment modernization.

Though one may argue whether a NATO country could involve Ukraine, a non-NATO state, into the modernization of its weapons, an example is already available. Croatia, a NATO member country since 2009, contracted Ukraine to modernize its Mi-8/17 helicopters and MiG-21 fighter jets. Ukraine's Ukrspetsexport reportedly won the contract against Russian, Belarusian and Czech firms. (Interfax-Ukraine, 2013)

However, it seems that this modernization potential has so far been considered in the Visegrad countries only to a very limited extent. In 2013 representatives of Poland and Ukraine discussed the possibility of Ukraine modernizing the Polish Air Force's MiG-29 fighters as well as the W-3PL multipurpose helicopters, but no decision has been made public so far. (Ukrainian Defense Review, 2013b)

Conclusion

Since its independence in 1991, Ukraine has consistently conducted a non-aligned, non-block foreign policy, and has not joined any of the regional security organizations such as NATO or the Collective Security Treaty Organization. This non-aligned security policy, however, has not prevented Ukraine from actively cooperating with the United Nations, NATO and the European Union.

Ukraine has been particularly active in the peacekeeping operations of the United Nations, and has so far acquired considerable crisis management-related knowledge and mission experience. Besides, Ukraine has been participating in all NATO ongoing operations, and Ukrainian units have contributed to the EU Police Mission to Bosnia-Herzegovina. Based on this accumulated mission experience, the well-trained, interoperable units of the Ukrainian armed forces indeed have the potential to become valuable partners of any CSDP crisis management operation, including those of the Visegrad Battle Group.

Moreover, Ukraine has considerable strategic airlift capabilities, something the CSDP has long been short of. Besides the well-known super heavy Antonov An-124 strategic airlifters that are regularly used by NATO in the framework of its Strategic Airlift Interim Solution (SALIS) program, Ukraine also has many Ilyushin Il-76 airplanes that are also suitable for supporting crisis management operations. This was recently put to the test in the framework of the Balkan Battle Group in 2011. Besides strategic airlift, the helicopter deployment potential of the Ukrainian air force should also not be forgotten. Ukrainian helicopters have been successfully serving in the UN missions to Liberia and the Ivory Coast, fulfilling both transport and combat support tasks.

In addition to all these, Ukraine's vast military industry potential would also offer numerous possibilities of cooperation with the EU, though these have so far not been taken up much. As there are still a high number of ex-Soviet military vehicles (tanks, armored personnel carriers, artillery pieces, etc.) in service in the former Warsaw Pact countries, there would indeed be room for Ukrainian defense industry companies to contribute to the modernization of these equipments. However, so far only a few, minor contracts have been signed, and Ukraine's potential for military equipment modernization is far from being fully utilized.

Bibliography

Alexandrov, O. (2012). Realities and prospects of Ukraine's cooperation with NATO in conditions of a non-bloc policy. *National Security & Defence.* 2/3 (131-132), 34-37.

Balcer, A. (2013). A Wishful Thinking? Military Cooperation in the Visegrad Group. Retrieved from http://visegradrevue.eu/?p=1437 . Visited 1.08.2014.

Black Sea News. (2014). Ukraine's Marines start HELBROC operational training. Retrieved from http://www.blackseanews.net/en/read/75193 . Visited 1.08.2014.

Bugriy, M. (2013). Strategic Incompatibility. *The Ukrainian Week.* Retrieved from http://ukrainianweek.com/Security/75910 . Visited 1.08.2014.

Central European Policy Institute. (2013). Visegrad Battlegroup. A Vehicle for Regional Defence Co-operation. Report from the DAV4 Visegrad Security Co-operation Workshop. Retrieved from http://www.cepolicy.org/sites/cepolicy.org/files/attachments/viseco_workshop_report.pdf . Visited 1.08.2014.

CMI. (2010). The Cockerill CT-CV (TM) Weapon System (advanced 105mm) successfully demonstrated its gun launched missile capability. Retrieved from http://www.cmi-groupe.com/en/news-view/191/the-cockerill-ct-cv-%28tm%29-weapon-system-%28advanced-105mm%29-successfully-demonstrated-its-gun-launched-missile-capability . Visited 1.08.2014.

Commission of the European Communities. (2003). Wider Europe – Neighbourhood: A New Framework for Relations with our Eastern and Southern Neighbours. Communication from the Commission to the Council and the European Parliament COM (2003) 104 final. Retrieved from http://eur-lex.europa.eu/LexUriServ/ LexUriServ.do?uri=COM:2003:0104:FIN:EN:PDF . Visited 1.08.2014.

Commission of the European Communities. (2004). European Neighbourhood Policy Strategy Paper. Communication from the Commission. COM(2004) 373 final. Retrieved from http://eur-lex.europa.eu/legal-content/EN/TXT/PDF/?uri=CELE X:52004DC0373&from=EN. Visited 20.08.2014.

European Union-Ukraine Summit. (2002). Joint Statement. Retrieved from http://europa. eu/rapid/press-release_PRES-02-195_en.pdf. Visited 20.08.2014.

Flightglobal Insight. (2013). World Airliner Census 2013. Retrieved from https://www. flightglobal.com/airspace/media/reports_pdf/world-airliner-census-2013-106686. aspx . Visited 1.08.2014.

Hungarian Presidency of the Visegrad Group. (Undated). Programme of the Hungarian Presidency 2013-2014 of the Visegrad Group. Retrieved from http://v4hupres.gov. hu/download/e/2e/70000/Program%20angol_v%C3%A9gleges.pdf . Visited 1.08.2014.

Interfax-Ukraine. (2013). Ukraine wins tender to repair Croatian MiG-21 fighters. Retrieved from http://en.interfax.com.ua/news/economic/158437.html . Visited 1.08.2014.

International Institute for Strategic Studies. (2013). *The Military Balance*. London: IISS.

Karlsson, N. (Undated). *EU Battlegroups – "Ambitious but rubbish?" Understanding the development of military capabilities within the ESDP from an institutional perspective*. Retrieved from http://lup.lub.lu.se/luur/download?func=downloadFile&recordOId=1520935&file OId=1520936 . Visited 1.08.2014.

Kuzio, T. (2003). EU and Ukraine: a turning point in 2004? (Occasional Papers No. 47). Paris: Institute for Security Studies.

Lindstrom, G. (2007). Enter the EU Battlegroups. (Chaillot Paper No. 97). Paris: Institute for Security Studies.

Lorenz, W. (2013). CEEDEFCO – A New Pillar of Ukrainian Defence. *PISM – The Polish Institute of International Affairs Bulletin*, 110 (563). Retrieved from https://www.pism.pl/ files/?id_plik=15048 . Visited 1.08.2014.

Ministry of Defence of Ukraine. (2014). БІЛА КНИГА 2013. ЗБРОЙНІ СИЛИ УКРАЇНИ [White Book 2013. Ukraine's Armed Forces]. Retrieved from http://www. mil.gov.ua/content/files/whitebook/WB_2013.pdf. Visited 20.08.2014.

Mission of Ukraine to the European Union. (2012). Foreign and security policy. Retrieved from http://ukraine-eu.mfa.gov.ua/en/ukraine-eu/dialogue/foreign-policy. Visited 1.08.2014.

Missiroli, A. (2003). The EU and its changing neighbourhoods: stabilization, integration and partnership. In J. Batt, D. Lynch, A. Missiroli, M. Ortega & D. Triantaphyllou, *Partners and neighbours: a CFSP for a wider Europe*. (Chaillot Paper No. 64, pp. 9-33). Paris: Institute for Security Studies.

NATO. (2004). NATO and Ukraine sign agreement on strategic airlift. Retrieved from http://www.nato.int/cps/en/natolive/news_20822.htm. Visited 20.08.2014.

NATO. (2014). Strategic Airlift Interim Solution (SALIS). Retrieved from http://www.nato. int/cps/en/natolive/topics_50106.htm?selectedLocale=en . Visited 1.08.2014.

NRCU. (2013). Ukraine to supply first mass-produced engine for new European Vega rocket in late 2013. Retrieved from http://www.nrcu.gov.ua/en/148/549158/ . Visited 1.08.2014.

Official Journal of the European Union. (2005a). Council Decision 2005/495/CFSP of 13 June 2005 concerning the conclusion of an Agreement between the European Union and Ukraine establishing a framework for the participation of Ukraine in the European Union crisis management operations. Retrieved from http://ec.europa.eu/world/agreements/downloadFile.do?fullText=yes&treatyTransId=2142. Visited 20.08.2014.

Official Journal of the European Union. (2005b). Council Decision 2005/481/CFSP of 13 June 2005 concerning the conclusion of the Agreement between the European Union and Ukraine on the security procedures for the exchange of classified information. Retrieved from http://eur-lex.europa.eu/LexUriServ/LexUriServ.do?uri=CELEX:32 005D0481:EN:HTML. Visited 20.08.2014.

Potapkina, V. (2010). Ukraine's Neutrality: A Myth or a Reality? Retrieved from http://www.e-ir.info/2010/11/30/ukraine%E2%80%99s-neutrality-a-myth-or-reality/ . Visited 1.08.2014.

SIPRI. (2012). Trade registers. Retrieved from http://portal.sipri.org/publications/pages/transfer/trade-register . Visited 1.08.2014.

SIPRI. (2013). The Top 20 Arms Exporters, 2008-2012. Retrieved from http://www.sipri.org/googlemaps/2013_of_at_top_20_exp_map.html. Visited 1.08.2014.

Strekal, O. (1994). The Ukrainian Military and Civil-Military Relations in the Post-Cold War Era. (INSS Occasional Paper No. 2). Colorado: US Air Force Academy, USAF Institute for National Security Studies.

Ukrainian Defense Review. (2013a). Ukrainian Helicopter: Dreams come true. 1, 48-53.

Ukrainian Defense Review. (2013b). Ukraine and Poland discussing defense-industrial cooperation. 4, 3.

Ukrinform. (2013). Ukraine will be invited to Visegrad Battlegroup. Retrieved from http://www.ukrinform.ua/eng/news/ukraine_will_be_invited_to_visegrad_battlegroup_302101. Visited 1.08.2014.

United Nations. (Undated). Troop and police contributors. Retrieved from http://www.un.org/en/peacekeeping/resources/statistics/contributors.shtml . Visited 1.08.2014.

Vlachos-Dengler, K. (2007). Carry That Weight. Improving European Strategic Airlift Capabilities. Retrieved from http://www.rand.org/pubs/rgs_dissertations/RGSD219.html . Visited 1.08.2014.

Worldwide News Ukraine. (2011). Ukraine Becomes the First Non-EU Partner to Join the EU's Military Peacemaking Force Stand-by. Retrieved from http://wnu-ukraine.com/news/politics/?id=436 . Visited 1.08.2014.

THE EU'S EXTERNAL ENERGY POLICY – FROM INTERNAL REFORMS TO FOREIGN POLICY

ANDRÁS DEÁK

Europe has the longest global record of dependence on energy imports. Since the emergence of crude oil as a major industrial fuel in the early 1900s, almost all European nations have been importing it on a large scale and have faced the foreign policy consequences of its domestic scarcity. This was not easy in an age of hegemonic aspirations. Churchill's efforts to establish a state-owned company (Anglo-Iranian, today British Petroleum) for the production of oil in then semi-colonial Iran, and Hitler's quest for synthetic petroleum and his military campaign for Baku, were rooted in the same strategic patterns. The rise of petroleum and motorization put a major strategic constraint and notion of vulnerability on European foreign policy mindsets in less than a generation's timeframe. Modern Europe has grown into energy dependency and it was in Europe that its significance was first demonstrated so spectacularly during the Second World War.

European energy relations thus became an important building block of the new, post-war security and political order, even if it was less visible than its other components such as the North Atlantic Treaty Organization (NATO) or Bretton Woods. Energy also played a vital role in the origins of the European Union (EU), long before the establishment of the European Economic Community (EEC). The first supranational institution on the path of European integration was the European Coal and Steel Community (ECSC), founded in 1951 by the Treaty of Paris. The primary policy rationale was one of security, i.e. of integrating Germany's heavy industry into a wider European region by barring the way to any potential rearmament effort. The single market was as much an international controlling mechanism over German industry as an economic instrument unifying European markets.

In the field of oil policy the post-war oil order was set up under the aegis of the United States (US). It aimed to channel American investments into the Middle East in order to secure supplies for reemerging European industries. These efforts stemmed as much from the US's geological constraints as from its economic and political aspirations. During the Second World War it became obvious that the European Allies could not fight a war without sizeable oil imports. Every second ton of shipment in the lend-lease program was of oil or oil products delivered primarily from and by the United States. By 1943 it became clear for the US's Petroleum Administration for War that the country did not have the oil reserves either for another world war or for supplying the globe after the end of the war. As Harold Ickes, chairman of the Petroleum Administration for War, declared publicly in 1943:

[I]f there should be a World War III it would have to be fought with someone else's petroleum, because the United States wouldn't have it... America's crown, symbolizing supremacy as the oil empire of the world, is sliding down over one eye. (Yergin, 1990, p. 395)

This recognition led to a conscious policy effort to set up a new supply framework in which Europe's oil security constituted the major driving factor. Europe's integration into the transatlantic security system was not manageable without solving its oil imports problem.

Due to these efforts, Europe's energy market integration was finalized by the mid-1950s. Coal and oil were practically the only fuels of industrial significance represented in foreign trade, providing around 85% of total primary energy consumption. The coal industry was integrated at the European level, while the oil sector was dominated by Western, predominantly American oil majors with liberalized investment and trade patterns. Major oil supply disruptions, which so often occurred between 1945 and early 1980s, were manageable in the system inherited from the Second World War and institutionalized as a response mechanism in the framework of the Organisation for Economic Co-operation and Development (OECD). This was an astonishing achievement, keeping in mind that in 1965 European energy consumption accounted for 26.2% of global supplies.

Figure 1. Europe's energy mix in historical comparison, in %

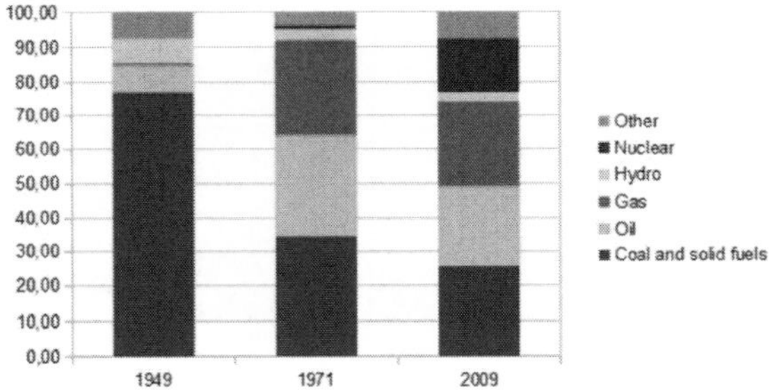

Source: United Nations, International Energy Agency.

This settlement had major ramifications throughout the international order. First of all, the post-war, bipolar Europe with its heavy load of hard security issues, provided a set of major political underpinnings. Both the Soviet threat and German integration were to be settled within a transatlantic framework, in which Europe had a significant role. The US airlift to Berlin in 1948 was just a small symbolic example of the broad energy guarantees provided by the US for Western Europe. Second, a third party was involved, the Middle East, where oil policy was heavily dominated by the US. Unlike in the mid-war period, Europe was no longer dependent so much on US oil imports, as on American concessions in the Middle East. Third, the settlement was only formed in the coal and oil segments, without any commitment to a further broadening of the scope. Other potential fuels, such as nuclear power or natural gas, were beyond the European and transatlantic energy sets. Since these fuels did not play a significant role prior to 1973, there was no need to form policy arrangements in these sub-sectors. None of these ramifications were present by 1989.

The 1973 oil crisis brought the first systematic attempt to establish a broad, European Community (EC)-wide energy policy. The embargo of oil supplies by the Organization of Arab Petroleum Exporting Countries (OAPEC) to some European countries created a challenge to solidarity within the EC and also brought into question the relevance of the existing transatlantic energy cooperation. The Commission faced a multi-faceted challenge, where it had all at once to increase the member states' solidarity and the EC's cohesion in the short-term, to develop long-term policy responses, and to manage the foreign policy consequences both in consumer-consumer and producer-consumer relations. It is worth underlining that, unlike with later attempts, these policies had only one goal, which was to improve the Community's energy security. No other sub-policies had to be harmonized with these priority considerations. Thus relatively early on, i.e. by the mid-1970s, the EC adopted a number of targets and formed a whole range of policies. These included an overall objective to reduce the share of imports to "50% and if possible 40%," and a commitment to increasing investments in nuclear energy to "at least 160 GW and, if possible, 200 GW;" a harmonized oil supply policy, later to be integrated into the International Energy Agency (IEA) regime established in November 1974; and a policy to foster dialogue with producers, especially to develop a "Euro-Arab" forum which would include energy on its agenda. (McGowan, 2011, p. 502-504)

Had these objectives been realized, the energy policy landscape of the EU would have developed dramatically differently during the 1980s. Nonetheless, the EC's institutional patterns were too weak to implement a functionalist leapfrog into energy policy at that time. This does not mean that European energy policies did not adapt to the new situation but that, in contrast to the Commission's proposal, the responses were much more national and mercantilist than collective and securitized. The structural change in the European energy market had been driven by the new price relations and implemented according to national preferences, rather than following a harmonized, common pattern.

Not surprisingly, the integrationist grip over EU energy markets weakened considerably by the second half of the Cold War: the change in the circumstances and the lack of will for adaptation made post-war energy policies obsolete. First of all, hard security considerations had lost some of their former relevance by the 1980s, paving the way for the comeback of economic and more market-oriented approaches. Energy issues had regained much of their former mercantilist nature. Germany was successfully integrated into the EC, while the US-Soviet *détente* provided an optimal framework for realignment in the economic sphere. Despite US opposition, West Germany and the Soviet Union broached the energy issue, laying the foundations for the current EU-Russia energy relations. At that time this was partly a diversification away from the unstable Middle East, and meant a broadening of the energy import portfolio. Energy never returned to being "just one of those commodities," but it was not a pure strategic asset anymore either.

Second, the 1973 and 1980 oil shocks also had a contradictory impact on European national policies. On the one hand it showed the limits of US influence on global oil issues and in the Middle East in particular, pushing the Europeans towards more autonomous, but not collective, responses. France's nuclear energy boom, Germany's gas imports from the Soviet Union, Dutch and North Sea developments all followed from the different global energy setup and price relations of the 1970s but showed a failure of EC members to develop harmonized national responses. In line with global trends, Europe turned to new fuels. Natural gas became the second most important fuel consumed in the EU by 1996, an amazing change from the early 1960s. Electricity markets have shown unprecedented growth since the 1950s.

As a result the European energy context became much more diversified both between suppliers and in particular fuels. It also led to a growing complexity of energy policies, showing much more sophistication than that of "domestic coal- Middle East oil" the 1960s. Many of these developments, and the gradual fragmentation of foreign energy relations, presented a new challenge to integration which European decision-makers left unanswered until the mid-1990s.

Thus the 1970s and 1980s brought a massive wave of renationalization of European energy policies. Since the post-war oil order and its linkages had been partially disrupted, security aspects related to coal gradually became irrelevant and European nations again established their own sectoral and foreign energy profiles. Germany, the United Kingdom (UK) and France's attitudes to external energy nonetheless differed from that of the US. The 1973 oil shock, the Arab embargo, the nationalization of US assets in the Middle East and the US's continued dependence on its supplies were a very new experience for Washington. This sectoral vulnerability, which was inseparable from its hegemony and superpower status, was thus perceived as a major foreign and security challenge. Europe had already experienced this vulnerability in the past. Its response was therefore much more functional, sectoral and based on the high level of interdependence with the suppliers. Until the late 1990s, Europe was the single most important global importer of energy, by far exceeding Japanese, US or Third World imports. This provided the old continent with a comfortable bargaining position. Interdependence was much less asymmetrical than it became in the 2000s.

The rebirth of a European energy policy after 1989 was very much a different matter. There was no specific external push to extend the acquis communautaire to this field. During the 1990s the international arena was peaceful, energy prices were moderate and economic growth relatively steady. In such an environment it was not a single leitmotif, especially not considerations of supply security, but a set of internal factors that triggered the rise of a common energy policy. (Faber Van Der Meulen, 2009, p. 842) The global liberalization of the energy sectors was one of the policy drivers. The decade brought a wave of privatization and market-oriented reforms not only in post-socialist Eastern Europe, but also in Latin America and even in the United States. This "policy fashion" very much inspired the European decision makers to launch a series of efforts aiming at the creation of an Internal Energy Market (IEM). Paradoxically enough the European gas and electricity single market effort was as much a liberalization process as a policy aiming to create an internal market. Its main ideological pattern was the abolishment of vertically integrated companies, creating liquid capacity- and commodity-trading schemes throughout the continent. It would be difficult to differentiate the goal and the instrument in this case. Critics often describe the European internal market as a purpose for itself. (Andoura, Hancher & Van Derwoude, 2010, p.30)

Another major development was the emergence of global environmental and climate policies. Two fundamental elements here were the EU Emissions Trading System (ETS) and a new Directive on Renewables (RES). (Wettestad, Eikeland & and Nilsson, 2012, p. 67) Paradoxically, even these originally had nothing to do with liberalization, as these policies had been running parallel for almost a decade without there being any significant links between the two. One reason for this was that climate policy had a much wider focus by default, covering all sources of greenhouse gas (GHG) emissions. However, ever since the EU took on its informal leading role at the Climate Change Convention in 1991 by pushing for the most stringent commitments, it became obvious that the two policy sets overlap. In the 1997 Kyoto Protocol the EU proposed the deepest emission cuts of all major industrialized nations. By 2007, with its 20-20-20 goal, the Community cemented its commitment and it became clear that the energy sector would have to make considerable contributions to climate change mitigation efforts.[1] This notwithstanding, leadership in global environmental governance and energy market liberalization are two rather different issues.

Supply security, which was originally subordinated to the IEM and RES policies without constituting an independent vector, is the most peculiar component of the EU's energy policy. As Francis McGowan stated:

> The Commission's 1995 White Paper on Energy Policy stated that, while growing energy dependency remained a concern "given the political risks in some important supplier countries" no new crisis measures were needed to address supply security issues. Throughout the period, moreover, the Commission argued that supply security would be best addressed through greater market integration, a reflection of the increased emphasis in EU energy initiatives on liberalisation and competition. (McGowan, 2011, p. 494)

However, by the mid-2000s supply security concerns reentered the EU energy policy debates. As early as 2005, the EC Green and White Papers drew the first outlines for an integrated energy policy, which derived the need for a common approach primarily from the changing global context and which put supply security concerns at a foremost place. (See Commission of the European Communities, 1995a; Commission of the European Communities, 1995b) In this sense supply security, even in the broader understanding, has been very much present independently of the new EU members' intentions. One of the major concerns is the EU's shrinking share in global energy demand: despite the steady growth of the last 50 years, the EU has recently accounted for only 13.4% of global consumption. Today the Far East, i.e. China and Japan, is the new powerhouse of energy imports, setting the scene for more competition and less international attention to the interests of the old continent. More globalized patterns of energy and the EU's shrinking role demand a more accommodating and responsive policy towards a larger array of fuels. Concomitantly the EU's overall import dependence is on an upward trend. The benefits of the last major oil and gas findings of the 1960s and 1970s in the Netherlands and the North Sea have been coming to an end. Between 2008 and 2013 the EU lost 25% of its natural gas production, pointing towards the growing significance of external suppliers in the future. European importers will have to compete for further imports in a more sophisticated and complex environment. All these considerations and projected challenges led to the rise of the common energy policy. The October 2005 Hampton Court summit recognized that:

> [the EU] needs to diversify [its] sources of energy and approach [its] current major energy suppliers in a more coherent manner; but it also need[s] to pursue energy efficiency and clean technologies and develop a genuinely open energy market. (Geden, Marcelis & Maurer, 2006, p. 10)

Still, the EU's newer members see supply security as a major concern, primarily with respect to gas supplies from Russia. It is true that the January 2009 Ukrainian-Russian gas price war was the most spectacular foreign energy policy crisis ever in Europe. The new member states

---

1   This shift is often described as a move from "directional leadership" to "leadership by example." (Oberthür & Roche Kelly, 2008)

have brought a noisy and very focused set of problems, namely the dependence on Russia in particular in the field of gas. Central and Eastern European (CEE) states put their problems at the top of their agenda, forming a small, but coherent and determined group and efficiently shaping the former *status quo*. However, as was shown above, old member states have had supply security in a broader sense since the origins of common energy policy, and this has never fully disappeared. In this regard the concern over the continent's capability to secure future supplies was a major factor of the reestablishment of the EU's energy policy. One reason why CEE countries' concerns could so swiftly penetrate the EU decision-making process was precisely their compatibility with the existing general setup of European energy security thinking.

Figure 2. The EU's share in global energy consumption, in Million tons of oil equivalent (Mtoe), 1965-2012[2]

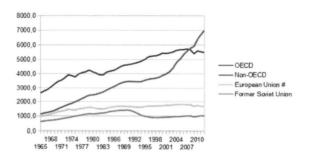

Source: BP Historical Review of World Energy.

The establishment of the legal basis of the EU's energy policy was finalized in the 2009 Lisbon Treaty with a specific Energy Title, transforming it into a full-fledged common policy on a normative basis. This policy's cohesion is nonetheless still on very shaky ground for a number of reasons. First, the high diversity of policy demand means the EU's energy policy has a wide range of objectives. Unlike in the 1970s, the goals of its three pillars (competitiveness, sustainability and supply security) are extremely stretched, importing a good deal of inconsistencies into the Union's policy. These three sub-policies are often perceived by stakeholders as contradictory and as decreasing the consistence of sectoral efforts. These objectives have not arisen simultaneously, as each goal was set independently without a deeper rethinking of the cumulative effects. Policies only partially overlap: the energy sector is only one segment of climate policy, while single market creation is limited only to two fuels. Until now the EU has rather drifted into energy policies, setting ever newer targets and broadening its scope with only limited success regarding a comprehensive ramification of its whole activity. Even on the theoretical level, it is questionable whether in the current technological matrix all these objectives can be achieved simultaneously and whether this option is optimal in a broader context.[3]

---

2   The EU excludes Estonia, Latvia and Lithuania prior to 1985 and Slovenia prior to 1991.
3   Evert Faber Van der Meulen, for instance, excludes the possibility of proper EU energy security policies due to its neoclassical regulatory features and lack of competences. (Van der Meulen, 2009, p. 843).

Figure 3. Self-sufficiency indicators of different fuels in OECD-Europe, in %, 1971-2008

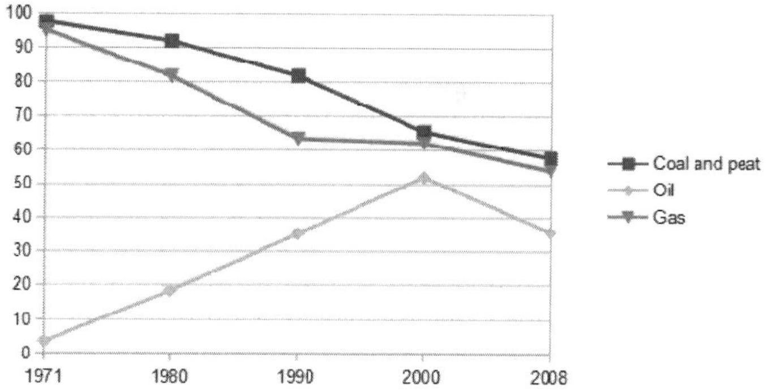

Source: International Energy Agency.

Second, EU energy policy involves a high number of different stakeholders. (On the complex institutional setting of the Energy Title under the Lisbon Treaty see Braun, 2011) National governments often perceive energy policy as a strategic issue, given the potentially enormous economic damage of any mismanagement or supply disruption in the sector. It is reasonable to say that, after defense policy, energy is the second most sovereign issue at the national level. Nation-states have withheld their sovereign rights to decide about the composition of energy mixes. This still opens up a wide range of different political patterns and social attitudes towards energy supply. Nuclear energy is a typical example where, for instance. Germany and France's approaches stand in total contradiction to each other, very much bringing into question the further deepening of the common policy. Corporate stakeholders also pose a number of challenges, since the sector is by nature oligopolistic with a small number of influential actors. Their decisions and reaction to common regulatory acts in the longer run may determine the future shape of European energy sectors. Furthermore, unlike the US which has minimal import dependence, the fate of Europe's energy landscape rests on a qualified number of external suppliers. Two major sets of policies, the IEM and the ETS-RES efforts, have far reaching consequences for the EU's external performance, putting additional emphasis on the management of external energy relations. Even if external actors do not have a say in the formulation of these policy sets, their level of cooperation and attitudes also influence the outcome, giving them an implicit say over the negotiation table.

Third, the sector has a growing number of sub-sectors and fuels, often requiring different approaches. Oil is traded on a liberalized global market, limiting potential intervention only to security and environmental standards. On the contrary, electricity and gas sectors are the main fields of common regulatory activities in which a single market is still to be established. However, these fields are precisely those most interconnected with other sub-sectors, generating a good deal of coordination tasks for any policy-driven intervention. RES and ETS policies, which provide the backbone of sustainability in the EU's approach, require an aggressive policy control over the market, annulling much of the liberalization mindset in the case of all other fuels' market.

Not surprisingly, at this stage the Union's energy policy has a strong internal focus. Brussels pursues a variety of unilateral functional and sectoral reforms, putting a large amount of emphasis on its external relations. Any unilateral change in the *status quo* causes further tensions in external relations. Despite its functional separation, the EU cannot un-bundle its external energy policies from the broader context of IEM, ETS-RES or competition activities. This is also partly due to the shortcomings of the external energy policy. Due to its under-institutionalization, the EU is unable or unwilling to communicate its internal actions externally. The embryonic common foreign policy cannot provide a strong internalization mechanism of external attitudes, channeling foreign interests into the decision-making process. Not surprisingly, the EU's external energy policy has a heavily biased record outside the Union. The countries of the Gulf Cooperation Council accused the EU of having an "overly narrow, regulatory-based approach to energy." (Prange-Gstöhl, 2009, p. 5297) Not surprisingly Algeria rejected the whole set of energy governance norms incorporated into the neighborhood action plan, and even friendly Kazakhstan, where the EU had high hopes of support, has resisted "an embrace of EU regulatory and market norms while it has no prospect of a place in the ENP [European Neighbourhood Policy]." (Ibid.)

It is not only a problem stemming from the EU's nature. In producer-consumer dialogues the EU's neoclassical liberalization model became to some extent "old-fashioned" in the midst of growing renationalization tendencies among the producer countries. Unlike in the 1990s, national oil companies (NOCs) solidified their domestic economic and financial foundations, shifting away from European models. (Umbach, 2010, p. 1232)

Even if producer-consumer (with Russia, Algeria, Qatar) or even consumer-consumer (with the US, China, Japan) dialogues are complex phenomena in international politics, often requiring hard policy instruments and a high level of political credibility, the challenge lies beyond these capability problems. This is a typical case of policy spillover, when internal actions have unintended or ignored implications in other fields, calling for further development of the EU's external energy policy during the 2000s. The EU's IEM, ETS-RES policies, as well as even some regional energy initiatives, by default affect its dialogues with other producers, and this often in a negative way.

Internal ramifications for energy policy – managing the policy gap

Thus the basic dilemma about external energy policy is one of whether it should be an extrapolation of EU internal policies, or some sort of energy-related track within the general external policy. Initial challenges and EU global aspirations would require the latter. In this case it would aim at full-fledged governance over international energy relations, similar to US foreign energy policy. This would require a realist approach to energy relations, aiming at maximizing the Union's benefits in some prioritized aspects. Nonetheless, the EU's existing internal capabilities, the functional *modus operandi* and its institutional ramifications underpin the former, functionalist approach, the creation and extension of the internal market to the neighboring environment, pursuing sustainability policies within the existing, rather narrow territorial coverage, and this only after managing the implications of internal actions on the relations with existing suppliers. The policy gap between the two models is relatively wide, which brings into question the credibility of the whole external action.

Large scale policy and regulatory resets are not unprecedented in energy policy history. Both the US and the United Kingdom reshaped their domestic policy settings in the field of natural gas and electricity during the 1980s and 1990s. In both cases this brought a longer period of uncertainty for market participants and business actors. In this regard both of these transformations demonstrate that external suppliers can tolerate these efforts and adapt to the new policy environment. At the same time it is worth highlighting some crucial differences. Both the US and the UK had a high level of self-sufficiency at that time, increasing the chance of higher legal coverage for the domestic regulator. Imports were only procured from Canada in the case of the US and from some marginal suppliers in the case of the UK. Climate policies were, furthermore, embryonic during these processes. By the time of the emergence of ETS-RES policies, the UK had already liberalized its domestic market, making its situation unlike that of the EU today. Finally, the wish to elaborate a high-profile external energy policy was absent during the liberalization process. Both the US and the UK had a well-established foreign energy policy, in particular oil policy, and did not harbor further external ambitions.

In the case of the EU the external and internal segments cannot be totally separated. External actors understandably exert considerable resistance against regulatory actions, with negative implications even on EU territory. Russia and Algeria have overtly ignored EU regulatory acts and found significant support for these positions among their trading partners. The case of the two Streams (Nord and South) and the implementation of the unbundling prescriptions (especially in the case of Lithuania) clearly show that external suppliers can influence the EC decision-making process and even recruit supporters among member states. It is even more difficult to expect Russia to accommodate its policy to the implementation of Energy Community requirements outside the Union, e.g. in Ukraine, if similar issues remain unsettled in EU-Russia bilateral relations. So long as global climate negotiations are not restarted and leading major industrial nations refuse to participate in them, climate change and energy efficiency measures remain an EU policy imperative for accession policies and an expectation *vis-à-vis* close partners in the neighborhood.

Thus the EU faces two interrelated challenges in its formulation of external energy policies. First, it has to drive its IEM and ETS-RES policies on an optimal path and towards an optimal and more advantageous target, keeping in mind the potential interaction with external suppliers. Second, it also has to prioritize between its external energy policy aspects and between goals existing in a complex set of interdependencies on the bilateral, regional and international levels. All this has to be done in an institutional landscape with many different fuels, actors and competencies.

Originally the external energy policy pointed more towards global aspirations than towards regional ambitions. The wish to create an external component, building up EU capabilities to speak with one voice to suppliers and other relevant actors, has been present since the "reestablishment" of a common energy policy. The Green Paper "A European Strategy for Sustainable, Competitive and Secure Energy" argues the need for an external energy policy in the following way:

> In order to react to the challenges of high and volatile energy prices, increasing import dependency, strongly growing global energy demand and global warming, the EU needs to have a clearly defined external energy policy and to pursue it, at the same time at both national and Community level, with a single voice. (Commission of the European Communities, 2006, pp.19-20)

Nevertheless, when it comes to details, the ambitious first list of tasks and targets towards such a policy provided in the document is of a partly different nature: identifying European priorities for the construction of the new infrastructure necessary for the security of EU energy supplies; developing a pan-European Energy Community Treaty; developing a new energy partnership with Russia; developing a new Community mechanism to enable a rapid and coordinated reaction to emergency situations in external energy supply impacting EU supplies; deepening energy relations with major producers and consumers; and reaching an international agreement on energy efficiency. On this basis the EU developed overlapping sets of instruments on the bilateral, regional and international levels. (Prange-Gstöhl, 2009)

Accordingly, the external energy policy became a coordinated policy between the member states. It was integrated into the general energy policy framework with its coordination cornerstone, the series of Strategic EU Energy Reviews. The task of the latter is to provide an overview of the energy situation in the Community and to set a regular framework of policy discussions, resulting in an updated set of measures, enabling more efficient common policy making. This notwithstanding, the formulation of the external energy policy has been delayed significantly. Unlike in all the other aspects of EU energy policy, external energy policy does not even have a basic legal setting yet.

This does not mean that there is no EU external action. If we look at the above-mentioned goals, formulated in 2006, the record is relatively positive. The European Energy Community is one of the key assets of the present external energy policy, going often hand-in-hand with accession, association and neighborhood policies and extending the zone of European regulation beyond the EU's borders. With a territorial extent covering not only all the Western Balkan states, but also Moldova and Ukraine, it bridges over accession and neighborhood countries. The separate institutional underpinning underlines the significance of energy during the takeover of the acquis. The Energy Community puts the sectoral integration onto a "fast track" of integration: by 2015 all these countries are to take over and implement the third or at least the second IEM energy package, much before other chapters of the acquis. In this regard it is right to describe this instrument as an exclusive asset of external energy policy, since legally it is not dependent on the accession pathways of these countries. A typical example is the TAP-pipeline, where the Energy Community provided a significant contribution by bringing the Albanian transit regulation in line with the European rules, independently from other sub-policies of the EU.

Again, the motivations of Community member states are rather diverse, putting EU regulation into different, sometimes highly politicized settings. Heiko Prange-Gstöhl provides three explanatory models for Community countries' acceptance of EU regulation without the immanent advantages of membership: the "identification motive", the "independence motive" and the "economic motive." (Prange-Gstöhl, 2009, pp. 5299-5300) While EU institutions often highlight the last motivation, namely that EU rules trigger more investments into these national sectors, the accession to the Energy Community is often interpreted in the member countries in the context of geopolitics or grand policy, as an instrument for fostering independence, strengthening the national bargaining positions vis-à-vis producers, in particular Russia. The EU's logic of unilateral regulatory arrangements by nature contradicts the bilateral contractual ramifications between Russia and post-Soviet states such as Ukraine or Moldova. Russia has put enormous effort into establishing a quasi-European contractual regime in the sphere of post-Soviet gas relations between 2005 and 2009. Understandably it interprets Energy Community membership as an attempt by the respective countries to reopen transit issues, this time with the institutional help of the EU. It doubts the regulatory commitment of these capitals, assesses these efforts as an attempt to repoliticize the relationship and clearly questions the EU's ability to control Ukrainian or Moldovan ambitions to abuse the EU acquis.

In these cases the EU and Russia have two parallel ideologies: the EU provides its unilateral regulatory model, while Russia insists on the preservation of the old European bilateral contractual relational *modus operandi* it has newly introduced in the post-Soviet space. This divergence of positions started long before the present decade, during the dispute over the Energy Charter Treaty (ECT) in the mid-2000s. Even if the ECT provided a high number of advantages for the Russian side, the latter refused to implement its provisions. (Konoplyanik, 2002, p. 630) This was partly due to its potential negative consequences in the sphere of Central Asian gas transit and domestic Russian investments, and to the high likelihood of the politicization of these particular issues. On the other hand Gazprom had reasonable doubts about the ECT's institutional capabilities and its applicability *vis-à-vis* post-Soviet transit countries. Some of these were justified later, after the accession of these respective countries and of Russia to the World Trade Organization (WTO), which provided no sizeable benefits in these disputes despite earlier hopes. In this context Gazprom trusted more old-fashioned contractual guarantees without open-ended international legal ramifications.

The EU policy vector and message to the transit states are also controversial. On the one hand it offers its policy toolkit with some technical and investment aid. It also pursues a policy of minimal or non-interference into Russia-Ukraine energy debates, taking them as business and bilateral issues. On the other hand, the 2009 Russia-Ukraine gas war contributed considerably to the elaboration of a more efficient emergency policy and of new security and regulatory standards for critical infrastructure. Many Eastern European countries experienced severe shortages at the time and their vulnerability was revealed in an obvious manner. All this led to the notion, gradually growing into an explicit recognition by 2014, that the CEE region needs additional interconnectivity and a harmonized development for its infrastructure. Since then the EU has built up significant financial, regulatory and technical capabilities fostering common infrastructural development. With the European Recovery Act and the Trans-European Energy Networks (TEN-E) programs, a new common instrument has been established with a significant coordination toolkit for future regional energy investments.

These policies have a dual nature. Four years later it is correct to say that this policy shows the beginning of a spillover into the neighboring regions. Western Balkan countries have started to identify projects of common interest, while reverse gas flows to Ukraine became an accessible option in less than two years. The dividing lines between EU and non-EU countries have lost some of their former significance with the development of many gas and electricity corridors connecting the two. Except for access to major development funds, non-EU markets are becoming increasingly similar to those of the member countries. The other side of the coin is that these efforts increase the EU's resilience to supply shocks and enhance the CEE states with more efficient response mechanisms. This undermines the bargaining position of the transit states *vis-à-vis* Russia and increases the likelihood of severe conflicts on the EU's periphery.

Nonetheless it is precisely these developments that have the least to do with the initial problem and respond to the challenge of the more globalized energy patterns. Common infrastructural development is primarily an internal, single market policy with some spillover into foreign trade. The Energy Community's highly visible pre-accession policy extends the acquis to the Balkans and to some countries in the Western Newly Independent States (NIS). Despite all these merits it would be difficult to argue that the Energy Community provides more leverage for the EU in global energy matters or that it sizably increases its energy security. Emergency policies are basically also internal instruments that can manage short-term disruptions and in many regards follow the models already established by the IEA.

The picture is much less positive if we look at the larger-scale goals. Relations with Russia have deteriorated since 2006. In 2000 the Green Paper "Towards a European strategy for the security of energy supply" characterized Russian dependence as "inevitable." (Commission of the European Communities, 2000) Describing the "continuity of supplies... over the last 25 years" as a "testimony to exemplary stability," it argued that a new partnership with Russia would enhance supply security. (Ibid.) By 2014 the Communication on European Energy Security Strategy set rather different tasks, such as "discussing with industry and Member States how to diversify crude oil supplies to EU refineries to reduce dependency on Russia" and manage the EU's Eastern member states' dependence on a single source of gas. (Commission of the European Communities, 2014, p. 11) It would be misleading to describe this trend as a failure exclusively on the part of the external energy policy. Nonetheless the Union's ability to set a uniform pattern of behavior with Moscow has increased only insignificantly. There is no convincing external policy argumentation even about the specific issues and severe conflicts of the EU-Russia relationship that originated from unilateral changes in EU energy regulations. As was the case with different IEM and RES targets directly affecting Russian plans and investments, it was the EU that changed the existing *status quo* without communicating on these developments with Moscow. Furthermore the EC's regulations and decisions by default involve competition policy aspects, implicitly distinguishing Russia negatively among suppliers due to its higher market share in many segments.[4] EU anti-trust investigations usually differentiate EU markets and set different benchmarks and different logics for national markets. Ever since the very beginning of the 2000s, the existing practice of IEM policy has been deeply questioning of the EU's energy partnership aspirations towards Russia.

There were, similarly, some sporadic efforts to establish communication channels with a selected set of countries and groups. EU-GCC (Cooperation Council for the Arab States of the Gulf, habitually known as the Gulf Cooperation Council) was one of the earliest examples, but similar separate forums for energy issues also exist at the EU-China and EU-Japan levels. Nonetheless these relations are heavily burdened both institutionally and by the lack of European authority. Energy is traditionally a bilateral issue, entrenched heavily beyond sovereignty. Without these capabilities, it is difficult to counterbalance the loss of Europe's share in global and Middle East energy trade and to compete with China, India, Japan or other importers with much bigger market potential and sizeable policy kits.

Bridging the policy gap is also to a great extent an internal EU institutional challenge. Theoretically external energy policy should bridge over the differences between energy and foreign policies, between the Directorate-General for Energy (DG Energy) and the European External Action Service (EEAS). The Commission has already developed significant leverage over internal energy matters: the third energy package and many environmental standards are already true common policies in which the member states have only limited say. External

---

4   Efforts to establish a single EU-Russia gas framework in the Russian understanding aim to destabilise Gazprom's system of long-term bilateral deals with European partners. (Yenikeyeff, 2006)

policies are much more harmonized, and in most cases their integration only started a couple of years ago. The EEAS does not have a considerable input into energy relations, and often duplicates or avoids energy issues in its activity. This fragmentation often handicaps relations with some suppliers, where energy is often the axis of any foreign policy activity. Despite the articulated significance of Azerbaijan as a new source of natural gas for Europe, energy was not represented in any other segments of the relations. Technical assistance and neighbor-hood policies were not coordinated with energy aspects, resulting in a serious loss of policy efficiency at the negotiations with Baku.

Thus the establishment of a strong EU external energy policy is also a matter of convergence. It has to provide both a solid vision for a future EU energy landscape and a reliable roadmap, and on this basis it has to prioritize its tasks with all the groups of external energy policy actors. All the disagreements between member states and inconsistencies between policy goals undermine primarily the external component and causing uncertainty among partners. Without a coherent set of policy goals, the external policy also will remain an in-coherent array of overlapping policies, discrediting in the longer run the EU's policy itself.

Different sets of partners

In its search for an efficient external energy policy, the EU has to cope with a high number of different partners. Its cooperation with the US in the framework of transatlantic relations is historically strong. It also has a distinguished set of suppliers of a different kind: Norway, which is virtually a member of the European energy space; Russia, a heavy-weight policy- and price-maker; some smaller suppliers such as Algeria, Libya and Azerbaijan, primarily all dependent on the European market; and producers with much less infrastructural and policy commitment to the old continent such as Qatar, Nigeria or Saudi Arabia. The neighboring regions, which are increasingly integrated into the Energy Community, the Western Balkans, and some Western NIS countries, pose a different challenge. At last the EC also strives to establish new policy channels with major global developing countries and organizations, such as China, India, Brazil or the Organization of the Petroleum Exporting Countries (OPEC), GCC and the Asia-Pacific Economic Cooperation (APEC). This is an extremely broad set of partners, a mix of bilateral and multilateral forums. In this section I will provide an overview of these relations and of the receptivity of different partners towards the EU.

As shown in the introduction, the transatlantic relationship has been Europe's longest-lasting and best source of energy cooperation. The US was the most important supplier of oil in the mid-war period and provided a strong security guarantee for European supply during the Cold War. Today's policy goals are very similar: the priority task of US foreign oil policy is to keep the global market well supplied, to explore and provide free access to foreign reserves, and to keep prices at a reasonable level. It has a strong liberal, free market-based ideology that very much appeals to the current European decision-makers. Both of these actors are industrially developed entities, and their foreign policy relations besides the energy sector are characterized by a relative degree of trust. US and European policy efforts overlap on a number of issues such as: the exploration of the Caspian basin and its opening to world markets; the consolidation of the Maghreb region and the preservation of these countries as reliable suppliers for Europe; the extension of European leverage in the neighboring regions and their integration into the European space; and the establishment of a balanced relationship with Russia and the preservation at a normal level of its leverage on European markets. Together the US and the EU have a greater chance of setting the global benchmarks and thereby of contributing to fostering the rules for the energy sector in the multilateral trade system. Institutional background and the potential for global governance are also sizeable: the International Energy Agency (IEA), the International Energy Forum (IEF), the International Partnership for Energy Efficiency Cooperation (IPEEC), and increasingly the G20 also provide important vehicles through which to influence the global energy debate.

At the same time, these relations have changed considerably since the end of the Cold War. First, they always had a slightly hierarchical nature. Primarily because of security considerations, the US provided the most important input into transatlantic relations. Second, Europe was, in global comparison, the biggest single entity importing oil and gas, thus influencing the market patterns significantly. Third, it was the perception of growing US dependency on imports that triggered the continuation of foreign policies and underpinned the US commitment to a bigger global representation. Today the policy settings for US foreign energy policies differ somewhat on all three points.

First of all, Europe has gradually been losing America's attention. This is a natural process, since the European continent succeeded in its consolidation following the break-up of the Soviet Bloc. There are no serious security challenges on the old continent (with to some extent an exception for Russia) and prolonged heavy-weight guarantees are no longer justified. This can be interpreted as a US call and also as an opportunity for a more autonomous European stance in global affairs, including in its own energy matters. Second, parallel to the general US turn towards the Far East, global energy balances have become much more dependent on the Pacific than on the Atlantic region. If it wants to keep energy markets consolidated, the US has to cope much more with China, Japan and India than with Germany, the UK or France. Unlike Europe, which has been dependent on energy imports since the late 19th century, many Asian societies have no experience with dependency. China started to import oil in 1995 and became the largest oil importer in less than two decades. Incumbent assertive energy policies and supply concerns are much more natural in such an environment with no tradition of global energy governance, than for the more relaxed European importer. The pacification and management of these emerging tensions are of much more vital importance to the US than is Europe's settled landscape.

Third and perhaps most importantly, the perceived US dependency path has been reversed. Due to a technological revolution and to "shale gas" and "tight oil" production, the US has a realistic chance of remaining self-sufficient in natural gas and of decreasing its dependency on foreign oil imports. If, ten years ago, the US was expected to become a major importer of Liquefied Natural Gas (LNG) on a global scale, today it is widely believed that the US will stop net imports and that it may become a sizeable exporter by 2020. According to IEA prognoses, US oil import dependency will continue to decrease from 45% in 2011 to only 34% in 2019. Apart from the positive implications on global energy balances, all these trends bring into question the nature of future US foreign energy policies. Prior to these developments, the US's growing activity, especially in the sphere of natural gas and LNG supplies, stems from the potential implications of global LNG scarcity on the US economy and on security itself. It was a sincere commitment rooted in mainstream American interests. Today gas prices at the US's Henry hub amount to only one-third of the average European level and global gas prices have no influence over US supplies.[5] It is mostly traditional US foreign policy, and not its energy policy component, that focuses on external gas issues today, greatly undermining the level of US commitment.

Figure 4. Global oil and gas dependency trends, 2010-2035

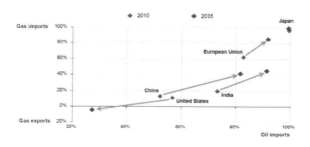

Source: International Energy Agency.

Paradoxically, these US trends favor the emergence of the EU's external energy policy. The Union has an opportunity to establish its own stance in a relatively peaceful market environment through a gradual and mutual decoupling from the existing patterns of transatlantic energy relations. It can preserve much of the existing relationship and formulate its own position on some particular issues. In a selected number of cases continuity will certainly prevail. The Transatlantic Trade and Investment Partnership (TTIP) is one of the opportunities to strengthen US-EU energy trade institutionally and to harmonize standards on the two sides of the Atlantic. Russian supplies, especially to Eastern Europe, will remain a key issue. Both the US and some CEE states are inclined to "securitize" the energy security narratives, resulting in the creation of some common ground and of a notion of better cooperation between them. The new EU members have already been capable of delivering a strong supply security message to Brussels and a few noisy Eastern European countries became the proponents of a one-voice policy, particularly towards Russia. The US seems to be highly supportive of diversification efforts in this region, primarily owing to security and political, rather than energy, considerations.

However, the biggest untapped potential in US-EU relations still lies in the climate change and environmental policy efforts. As in the field of energy, transatlantic cooperation on environmental issues was very strong until the early 1990s. Since then both sides have followed an increasingly divergent path culminating in the US's withdrawal from the Kyoto Protocol in 2001. (Vandeveer, 2009, p. 42) This was a major blow for Europe's governance leadership attempts and showed the limits (and to some extent the asymmetry) of transatlantic relations. US opposition resulted in the EU's failure to get the critical support to establish a consolidat-

---

5   The US can provide some LNG supplies to the old continent but this is more a commercial issue than a political one. Nonetheless some minor political steps have been taken: the Congress for instance gave member states of the North Atlantic Treaty Organization (NATO) the same status as free trade countries with regard to possible US LNG exports. (Ratner, Belkin, Nichol & Woehrel, 2013, p. 5)

ed climate change stance among major industrialized countries. This weakened the credibility of global climate governance at the UN negotiation table, where North-South divisions are of primary importance. The EU remained alone and had to launch its own, individual emission reduction system (ETS) in order to keep alive the image of its global climate leadership.

This fiasco is less substantial and more diplomatic than it seems to be. Since then the US has started to reduce its emissions and, in retrospect, it could have joined the Kyoto Protocol with moderate economic sacrifices. On a purely statistical basis, the US and the EU have the best records globally in emission reductions in the last five years. The US has decreased its GHG-emissions by 8% between 2007 and 2011 and its level is less than in 2001, when the US Congress refused to ratify the Kyoto Protocol. (US Environmental Protection Agency, 2013) But the precedent, demonstrating the full commitment of industrialized nations, had not been delivered and the EU could not sustain the credibility of the Kyoto system with its *ad hoc* coalition, supported by Russia. The transatlantic relation failed to establish the essential narrative and the industrialized nations to speak with a common voice to persuade developing countries to enter into further commitments, thus contributing to the collapse of global climate change negotiations in 2007.

There is a wide variety of external suppliers in EU energy relations. Their status differs on all possible counts, including in their institutional background, levels of commitment, nature and coalitions. In global comparison the structure of import sources is relatively concentrated: Norway and Russia deliver two-thirds of the EU's total gas imports and almost half of its oil imports. The US, as well as most of the Far Eastern countries, pursue some sort of portfolio diversification policy in their imports and have more balanced sets of exporters. From the theoretical point of view a centralized EU system could lead to the creation of a more balanced set of importers and improve the position of Europeans at the negotiation table.

Figure 5. Sources of oil and gas imports to the EU, in %, 2009

EU imports of natural gas, by country of origin in 2009			EU imports of crude oil, by country of origin in 2009		
Country:	Import %		Country:	Import %	
Russian Federation	34.00		OPEC	35.00	
Norway	31.00		Russian Federation	33.00	
Algeria	14.00		Norway	15.00	
Qatar	5.00		Kazakhstan	5.00	
Libya	3.00		Azerbaijan	4.00	
Nigeria	2.00		other	8.00	
Egypt	2.00				
other	9.00				

Source: Europe's Energy Portal.

The EU has a relatively heavy load of issues in the producer-consumer dossiers. Most of these stem from the Union's striving for setting new rules for suppliers. Brussels expects normative adaptation in the broader sense to European legislation, the implementation of the third package by exporters in EU territory, and for the new hub pricing benchmarks in the supply contracts to be respected. Understandably the emergence of these issues is a direct result of unilateral EU actions and puts these relations under serious stress. Non-fulfilment requires legal sanctions from the Union's side in most of the cases, while some issues such as gas pricing remain in an uncertain legal limbo, where competition rules are often applied. In addition to these, other EU measures often distort market relations in an unpredictable way.

Uncertainty about emissions trading, and a high number of different environmental targets applied very differently by member states, all pose investment risks for exporter companies and consequently for the supplier governments. These issues are not even on the negotiation table as they constitute normal investment risks for most of them.

The high number of unilateral issues raised by the EU brings into question the existing *status quo* of these relations. Providing an efficient framework for energy relations between the EU's member states and energy supplying countries can best be achieved by recognizing "mutual interdependency" as the starting point, as the EU cannot go beyond certain limits. It is a classic prisoner dilemma: if these relations can be managed only mutually and energy security is a "common good," individual strategies can only be pursued beneficially so long as the other side does not take action in response. The EU's internal focus failed to integrate relations with exporter countries, and this missing link may lead to sub-optimal results if external suppliers also opt for individual optimization strategies. The problem is more acute if we look at the *sui generis* nature of climate change and single market policies, where security of supply is not a major factor for consideration. The question is whether EU non-inclusion policy can provide better energy security if mutual interdependency is present.

Non-inclusion does not presuppose neutrality. The EU identifies itself as a promoter and supervisor of competitiveness on its own internal market. From this position it may differentiate between suppliers according to their contribution to market relations on the whole or to particular market segments. It differentiates between better and worse suppliers indirectly, through competition rules. But competition rules means differentiation, and differentiation presupposes a carrot and stick strategy. Unlike for South Stream, the TAP pipeline was exempted from capacity allocation because it brings gas from new sources to the market. Norwegian gas has a better regulatory environment than the Algerian, since the marketing characteristics of the former are more conform to EU requirements. Adaptation has its reward, even if formal negotiations are absent between the sides.

Not surprisingly there is a high variety of supplier strategies and adaptation paths. Norway, a relatively new exporter nation with very strong infrastructural connections to Europe, chose to take a cooperating stance with a swift acceptance of new EU norms. This was not so obvious given the complex Norwegian record of producer-consumer cooperation with the EC in the past. Norway has cautiously distanced itself from past European attempts to create a common energy area. During the 1980s the "blond Arabs" supported the OPEC's quota policy and cut back their oil production several times in order to enable a more efficient OPEC price setting. At the beginning of the 1990s Norway pulled back from the Energy Charter Treaty, a European effort to extend a set of sectoral liberalization measures throughout the continent. The document was by far too "consumer-oriented" for an exporter country where rents and sovereignty over national resources are still a matter of national interest. These were pragmatic national choices, often legitimized by the local parliament in a highly democratic manner.

Norway's membership of the European Economic Area (EEA) nonetheless provided it with a degree of leverage on some of these energy-related issues. Since the EEA's creation in 1994, Norway has a soft capability to influence European decision making and a better bargaining position on the implementation of new EU rules. Unlike other exporters, Norway and Norwegian companies have an early-warning system within the Commission and can shape both the decisions and their own national policies according to the changing environment. Norway received a high number of exemptions during the implementation of former energy packages and it has recently been moving towards hub pricing in its export contracts. Thus it is highly questionable whether Norway can be included as a subject of external energy policy. In reality, EU-Norway relations presuppose a good deal of inclusion, making this case rather more special than normal.[6]

Russia is the single biggest issue for external energy policy. Given its robust share in the Union's imports, its dominance over the Eastern gas markets, its broad range of different exports stretching from nuclear energy and coal to electricity and hydrocarbons, and its overall significance for the EU's external relations as such, Russia is the cornerstone of any thinking about common energy actions. Many actors see it as a symbol of monopolism, vertical integration, political misuse of energy and geopolitical extension, yet Russia is at the same time the biggest potential prize for EU energy relations: a powerful ally strongly interdependent with European markets and a last resort for incremental supplies and external help in case of a sharp deterioration in the global energy situation. EU-Russia relations have solid foundations but also a volatile mutual perception.

The past two decades have been an excellent illustration of these trends. Energy trade between the EU and Russia has grown in a robust manner since 1991, increasing the EU's dependence on Russian energy, and Moscow's both on energy exports and on Europe. Russia has as good as become an oil-state with the wider Europe almost exclusively as its export market. However, the rise in trade was not accompanied by growing trust at a satisfactory level. Neither side could separate the transformative aspect from energy relations. Accordingly, when Russia showed increased affinity to market reforms and democratic development, as it did in the early 1990s and early 2000s, attempts were made towards establishing some sort of multilateral governance. But deterioration in foreign policy relations caused geopolitics to prevail, leading to serious conflicts, as was the case during the second half of the 2000s. As Kirsten Westphal put it:

> What has become apparent (again) over recent years is the fact that energy governance takes place in a field of tension between governance based on market and institutions (and the rule of law) on the one hand, and state-centered, power-based geopolitics on the other. The latter represent spaces dedicated to accumulating influence. They are structured by hegemons and thus capable of resulting in regional blocs and "empires" ... The multilateral governance approach aims to manage interdependence on the basis of anonymously and equally applied rules and an access to resources and investment moderated by market mechanisms, along with strong involvement of private companies. The geopolitical pattern seeks to secure exclusive access to resources, mainly by political and military means. (Westphal, 2007, p. 58)

The main dilemma nonetheless is whether there can be some common ground between these two ideologies. Sanam Haghighi argues that the middle ground exists in the form of a triangular "commercial-development-foreign policy" approach, where energy security can only be achieved by integrating the three above-mentioned aspects of the picture. (Haghighi, 2007, p. 480) This would mean a broad approach, more mercantilist than the EU's position today, but to some extent still with political content through foreign policy representation. At the same time this presupposes a step beyond the current functionalist-sectoral approach and

---

6   Also important is that Norway perceives the single European market as a goal of interest and supports it. (European Economic Area, 2012, p. 9)

multilateral governance efforts. The last attempt to establish a pan-European energy community in 2006 was elaborated in this later context. It repeated the basic patterns of previous institutional efforts. In this regard the 1994 European Charter Treaty to some extent still determines the EU's way of thinking, with integration and liberalization at its core.

This notwithstanding, the European Charter Treaty was the most comprehensive attempt to create a pan-European energy landscape on a multilateral basis. Since then the relations have been becoming gradually more bilateral, the scope more narrow and the topics more selected. Insistence on Russian ratification of the Treaty slowly became a barrier and its vivid memory poisoned the relations between the two neighbors. The Treaty was out of reach as early as 2003, but it took another couple of years to admit this at the official level.[7] The substitution to ECT was integrated into the four EU-Russia "Common Spaces," where energy became one of the highlighted issues, and the EU-Russia Energy Dialogue.[8] Nonetheless these instruments never became hard policy instruments and were rather some sort of consultative bodies without any particular target or solid goals.[9] Accordingly, these institutions were not capable of managing the tensions of the second half of the 2000s, when Russia even started elaborating and proposing alternative solutions to existing problems.

EU market reforms and the call for Russian accommodation can be interpreted as a unilateral effort to push Russian energy policy towards partial integration. In this regard the shift in the bilateral relations is not a matter of policy scope, but a move away from bilateral solutions towards enforcement, even if only on some selected questions. The short-term market situation in the field of natural gas favors these attempts. The buyers' market in Europe puts existing Russian contracts and marketing strategies under stress and forces Gazprom to serious concessions. At the same time unilateral steps open up the way for Moscow to choose the form of its own adaptation. Diversification away from European markets has been accelerated by European trends and the long-term flexibility of Russian producers is becoming increasingly questionable. Surprisingly it was the EU that launched the unbundling process in EU-Russian relations, after assessing Russia's share of European markets as too large. The future form of the relations and the long-term implications of this policy remain to be seen.

In light of the high proportion of Russian and Norwegian imports, all other sources remain alternative and strengthen diversification. Size matters, and this influences EU attitudes towards suppliers. While Gazprom made a significant number of concessions to EU policies and showed a considerable degree of adaptation, it received much more criticism and scrutiny than Algeria's Sonatrach with its rigid pricing and contractual framework. Azerbaijan, with its poor record on human rights and democratic values, remains among the countries favored by DG Energy and many national capitals. This is understandable given the complexities of EU decision making and the logic of energy policies. What is more, the nature of the Euro-Mediterranean partnership and to some extent of EU-Azeri relations means transformative aspects tend to be superseded by mercantilist attitudes. This is a political concession to these suppliers, who do not differ substantially from Russia in their dependence on the European

---

7   Poland has its own position on this particular "energy partnership" with a focus on ECT. (See Geden, Marcelis & Maurer, 2006, p. 23-24).

8   Some elements were incorporated from ECT into these instruments by the EC, but with little success. (Müller-Kraenner, 2010, p. 3).

9   Russia offered to "harmonize" its relations with European actors, while the EU insisted on "exporting" its acquis at the bilateral level. (Konoplyanik, 2008).

market and their ambitions to take over the Union's standards. Theoretically the EU could establish increased policy benchmarks through its energy policy *vis-à-vis* these countries, due to their smaller significance in European supplies and of the larger relative share of energy exports for their gross domestic product. However, purely from the point of view of energy, the nature of these states' energy policies is not very relevant so long as they are ready to deliver their production to European markets. In the EU context the characteristics of Algerian, Libyan or Azeri supplies are much closer than Russia's to the conventional energy supplier logic.

The challenge for Europe's relation with these countries is much more a conventional security issue than a simple energy one. Energy is a major stake in the stability *vs.* democracy dilemmas regarding the region. The consequences of the Arab Spring in the Maghreb, Egypt, Libya and potentially even Algeria are becoming one of the major challenges for EU oil and gas security. The collapse of the Mubarak and Gaddafi regimes and the growing paralysis of the Algerian government are putting investments and even the reliability of uninterrupted supplies at imminent risk. Libyan exports have been regularly halted or have decreased since the fall of the Gaddafi regime, Algerian energy exports are heavily constrained by severe underinvestment, and Egyptian riots and instability threaten the normal functioning of the Suez Canal. All these problems go beyond the sectoral logic and cannot be managed by sectoral instruments. It is a political issue that may require a comprehensive consolidating approach from European actors.

In this respect energy security issues constitute just another cause for rethinking the EU's Mediterranean policy and taking on a greater engagement in the region. Energy is another major issue in regional policy beside other major threats such as migration, refugees and terrorism. In view of the current market situation, the loss of a supplier is manageable. Oil markets are relatively relaxed and gas supply cuts can be offset by other imports, including from Russia or of LNG. The Mediterranean region provided only 11% of total EU gas consumption in 2012. But together with other factors it puts a significant pressure on European policies and cannot be left without response in the future. In this regard energy cannot be separated from the complex regional landscape and stable supplies remain a major benefit for the EU.

Relations with other partners such as GCC, the Association of Southeast Asian Nations (ASEAN), Japan or China do not form a single, coherent set. The EU launched these institutional dialogues at different times and for various reasons. The policy coupling has never been strong and energy has never represented a major issue except perhaps in relation with the Gulf Cooperation Council. Emerging multilateral tracks such as G20, global climate change negotiations and even UN organizations pose a significant competition to any of these institutions. Apart from the trade issues, it is in many cases only the global supply-demand balance that brings these countries together. The "consumer camp" traditionally has been led by the US, which has a long record of global oil and to some extent gas governance. In this regard these horizontal relations are often secondary for both sides. EU climate change policy leadership could have justified many of these channels, some of which were launched precisely at that time, when the EU made efforts in such a direction. However, due to the decline of these UN negotiations, energy ceased to be a significant issue in most of these Far Eastern relations.

Conclusion

The EU's external energy policy has developed since the mid-2000s in a situation of growing scarcity and competition for global energy. Still, unlike in the 1970s, there have been no major supply security challenges on the economic-political horizon. The gas supply crisis of 2009 was a relatively low-profile event if compared to the oil shocks of 1973 or 1979-80. Consequently, the global energy patterns has only a moderate impact on external policies, leaving more room for internal considerations and factors. In this regard the future of the EU's external energy policy to a large extent depends on the global energy landscape and on the EU's internal ambitions. If the global, and in particular the European energy security landscape remains geopolitically calm and reliable, the European actors will be able to continue its gradual development. In all other cases Europe will have to face a situation in which it will have to rely more on its own resources and potential than in the past.

Bibliography

Andoura, S., Hancher, L. & Van Derwoude, M. (2010). *Towards a European Energy Community: A Policy Proposal*. Notre Europe. Retrieved from http://www.europarl.europa.eu/meet-docs/2009_2014/documents/envi/dv/201/201006/20100602_envi_study_energy_policy_en.pdf. Visited 04.10.2013.

Braun, J. F. (2011). EU Energy Policy under the Treaty of Lisbon. Rules between a new policy and business as usual. (EPON Working Paper No. 31). Retrieved from http://www.ceps.eu/book/eu-energy-policy-under-treaty-lisbon-rules-between-new-policy-and-business-usual. Visited 1.10.2013.

Commission of the European Communities. (1995a). For a European Union Energy Policy – Green Paper, COM(94) 659.

Commission of the European Communities. (1995b). An Energy Policy for the European Union – White Paper, COM(95) 682 final. Retrieved from http://europa.eu/documentation/official-docs/white-papers/pdf/energy_white_paper_com_95_682.pdf. Visited 14.08.2014.

Commission of the European Communities. (2000). Towards a European strategy for the security of energy supply – Green Paper, COM(2000) 0769 final. Retrieved from http://eur-lex.europa.eu/legal-content/EN/TXT/HTML/?uri=CELEX:52000DC0769&from=EN. Visited 16.07.2014.

Commission of the European Communities. (2006). A European Strategy for Sustainable, Competitive and Secure Energy – Green Paper COM(2006) 105 final. Retrieved from http://europa.eu/documents/comm/green_papers/pdf/com2006_105_en.pdf. Visited 14.08.2014.

Commission of the European Communities. (2014). European Energy Security Strategy. Communication from the Commission to the European Parliament and the Council. COM(2014) 330. Retrieved from http://ec.europa.eu/energy/doc/20140528_energy_security_communication.pdf. Visited 17.07.2014.

European Economic Area. (2012). Joint Parliamentary Committee. Report on the future of the EU Energy policy and its implications for the EEA. Retrieved from http://www.efta.int/media/documents/advisory-bodies/parliamentary-committee/jpc-reports/EEA_JPC_Report_Energy_Policy.pdf. Visited 3.10.2013.

Faber Van der Meulen, E. (2009). Gas Supply and EU-Russia Relations. *Europe-Asia Studies.* 61(5), 833-856.

Geden, O., Marcelis, C. & Maurer, A. (2006). Perspectives for the European Union's External Energy Policy: Discourse, Ideas and Interests in Germany, the UK, Poland and France. (Working Paper FG 1, 2006/17). Berlin: Stiftung Wissenschaft und Politik.

Haghighi, S. (2007). *Energy Security – The External Legal Relations of the European Union with Major Oil and Gas Supplying Countries.* Oxford: Hart Publishing.

Konoplyanik, A. (2002). Rossiyskiy vzglyad na Evropeyskuyu Eenrgeticheskuyu Hartiyu in Dogovor k ney do i v processe peregovorov [Russian view on the European Energy Charter Treaty before and during the negotiations]. In A. Konoplyanik, *Dogovor k Energeticheskoy Hartii: put k investiciyam i torgovle dlya Vostoka i Zapada* [The Energy Charter Treaty: road to investments and trade between the East and the West] (pp. 138-163). Moscow: Mezhdunarodniye Otnosheniya.

Konoplyanik, A. (2008). Regulating energy relations: *Acquis* or Energy Charter? In K. Barysch, *Pipelines, politics and power. The future of EU-Russia energy relations* (pp. 107-115). London: Centre for European Reform.

McGowan, F. (2011). Putting Energy Insecurity into Historical Context: European Responses to the Energy Crises of the 1970s and 2000s. *Geopolitics.* 16, 486-511.

Müller-Kraenner, S. (2010). *The external relations of the EU in energy policy.* Heinrich Böll Stiftung. Retrieved from http://www.boell.de/de/node/275156. Visited 17.09.2013.

Oberthür, S. & Roche Kelly, C. (2008). EU Leadership in International Climate Policy: Achievements and Challenges. *The International Spectator: Italian Journal of International Affairs. 43(3), 35-50.*

Prange-Gstöhl, H. (2009). Enlarging the EU's internal energy market: Why would third countries accept EU rule export? *Energy Policy.* 37(12), 5296-5303.

Ratner, M., Belkin, P., Nichol, J. & Woehrel, S. (2013). *Europe's Energy Security: Options and Challenges to Natural Gas Supply Diversification.* Congressional Research Service. Retrieved from http://fas.org/sgp/crs/row/R42405.pdf. Visited 11.10.2013.

Umbach, F. (2010). Global energy security and the implications for the EU. *Energy policy.* 38(3), 1229-1240.

US Environmental Protection Agency. (2013). Inventory of U.S. Greenhouse Gas Emissions and Sinks: 1990-2011. Washington: US Environmental Protection Agency. Retrieved from http://www.epa.gov/climatechange/ghgemissions/usinventoryreport.html. Visited 21.07.2014.

Vandeveer, S. D. (ed., 2009). *Transatlantic Environment and Energy Politics: Comparative and International Perspectives.* Burlington, VT: Ashgate Publishing.

Westphal, K. (2007). Energy Policy between Multilateral Governance and Geopolitics: Whither Europe? *Internationale Politik und Gesellschaft.* 4, 44-62.

Wettestad, J., Eikeland, P.O. & Nilsson, M. (2012). EU Climate and Energy Policy: A Hesitant Supranational Turn? *Global Environmental Politics.* 12(2), 67-86.

Yenikeyeff, S. M. (2006). *The G8 and Russia: Security of Supply vs. Security of Demand?* Oxford Energy Comment. Retrieved from http://www.oxfordenergy.org/wpcms/wp-content/uploads/2011/01/August2006-TheG8andRussia-ShamilYenikeyeff-.pdf. Visited 29.09.2013.

Yergin, D. (1990). *The Prize: The Epic Quest for Oil, Money & Power.* New York: Free Press.

MIGRATION: CHALLENGE OR OPPORTUNITY?

BÉLA SOLTÉSZ

International migration is a complex phenomenon that has been approached by practically all the branches of the social sciences. Theorizing migration is, therefore, an intellectual building of bridges between different disciplines: depending on the concrete question, one can easily arrive at different realms. The root causes of migration are, for instance, mostly investigated by economics, while the concrete migratory process and the inclusion or exclusion of migrants in the receiving country is a field of study for sociology and anthropology. Regulating migratory flows is a problem that belongs to law and political science, while the long-term developmental effects of migration are observed by scholars of demography and, again, economics. Finally, history and geography also have their say when it comes to concrete spatial and historical analysis. (Massey et al., 1993; Brettel & Hollifield, 2008; de Haas, 2008)

This multi-focality can, however, be simplified to some extent, as the approach and aim of analysis are similar in different disciplines. First, economics and demography are interested in the overall process of migration and have a rationalist approach, seeing the individual migratory decision as utility-maximizing behavior. Migration is here seen as a macro-level process that is a sum of individual responses to a developmental challenge, that is, the difference in wages and living standards between different countries. The impact of migration on the population's size, structure and economic performance are the main concerns, thus it can be labeled the *development approach*.

Second, sociology and anthropology have a structuralist rather than a rationalist approach. As opposed to neoclassical economics' micro and macro theories that focus on labor supply and demand, several theories elaborated by from sociologists and anthropologists underline the embeddedness of migration in a wider societal context. Network theory and cumulative causation theory, for instance, see migration as part of an adaptation process of the individual to the structures of inclusion and exclusion, rather than as an economically rational choice. The main concern of these currents of thought is how migrants can be incorporated into the migrant-receiving country and what social and cultural challenges this implies, therefore it can be called the *integration approach*.

Third, law and political science have an institutional approach, focusing on the state and its institutions that define the outlines for regulating migration. Questions of sovereignty and control are at play, i.e. how undesired migrants can be kept out and desired migrants can be let in, in an otherwise liberal state that respects the civil rights of the individuals staying on its territory. This approach is a normative one, and is linked to the concept of security, which understands migration as a challenge for legislation, police and border patrol bodies. In many ways, the refugee question also belongs to this realm, which can be labeled the *security approach*.

Regarding the question posed in the title of the present chapter, an interesting bias can be detected in the three approaches described above. The security approach focuses mostly on the challenges, while the integration approach underlines the opportunities that a migrant population yields. In many ways, understanding migration as a process that the state cannot control properly determines a vision of the issue as a "challenge", while the integration approach, i.e. seeing migrants as a structurally disadvantaged social group whose capabilities are not used properly by the migrant-receiving society, opens the path for a vision of "opportunity." Contrary to these two, the development approach is more keen on listing challenges and opportunities in the same conceptual framework, as its hypothetical actor is a fully rational individual (or group of individuals) that evaluates costs and benefits before taking the migratory decision. Although this approach also has its shortcomings, it is still the most convenient for the purposes of this chapter. In the following, therefore, a developmental perspective on migration will be adopted, without losing sight of some of the other two approaches' important points.

That being said, it is of particular importance to look at how migratory trends have shaped Europe's population in the past centuries. As mentioned before, migration case studies rely heavily on history and geography, and in the European case it is also crucial to understand the temporary and spatial dimensions of the process. From a spatial point of view, this chapter considers the "wider Europe" as its subject, with special attention being paid to the differences between Western and Eastern Europe regarding their role in the migratory processes.

Migration and policy making in Europe: from "historical ties" to "global cities"

Throughout the largest part of its modern history, Europe was a migrant-sending continent. European colonization was driven primarily by demographic surplus, and the independence of settler and creole nations in the Americas and in Australia did not stop the process but rather accelerated it. Until the economic boom of the 1960s in Western Europe, it was much more likely for a European to migrate to a non-European country than for a non-European to migrate to Europe. Intra-European migration, however, was a very common feature, either for economic reasons (German *Aussiedler* in Eastern Europe from the Middle Ages to the early 20th century, Polish and Italian guest workers in France in the 19th century etc.) or for political ones (French Huguenots throughout Europe in the 18th century, Greek, Turkish, German, Hungarian etc. subjects of population transfer agreements following the First and Second World Wars etc.). (Sassen, 1999)

The major turning point for these trends came in the 1960s, for three reasons. First, political stability was achieved and during three decades and a half (between the 1956 revolution in Hungary and the Yugoslav wars starting in 1991) no major refugee wave originated from within Europe. Second, with the dismantling of the colonial empires, a large number of the descendants of European settlers moved back to Europe, followed by an equally large number of migrants of non-European or mixed ancestry. (Joppke, 2005) Third, economic growth and the rise in living standards caused a demand for manual workers in many Western European countries with no post-colonial immigrant population, such as Germany, Switzerland or Sweden, that actively recruited guest workers in countries whose governments readily signed bilateral treaties in order to set the legal framework for these, suppos-edly circular, migratory movements. Labor-exporting countries included, among others, Turkey, Yugoslavia, Spain and Portugal: in Wallerstein's definition, these were "the whole outer rim of Europe" or the European semi-periphery, excluding the members of Council for Mutual Economic Assistance (COMECON) where mobility was restricted. (Wallerstein, 1979, p. 100)

Post-colonial migration relied on a previously established asymmetrical relationship be-tween European and non-European territories, euphemistically called "historical ties." Either because of a sheer economic rationale or an ideological mixture of belonging, historical guilt and paternalism, countries such as the United Kingdom (UK), France, the Netherlands, Spain and Portugal provided preferential terms of entry for the citizens of their ex-colonies. (Joppke, 2005) Contrary to this, the guest worker-receiving countries listed above did not have any historical or cultural ties with the sending countries, and the whole process was intended to be temporary and strictly labor-driven. However, as Swiss novelist Max Frisch put it in an oft-quoted sentence, "we asked for workers and we got people instead." (Cited in Hollifield, 2006, p. 183) Many guest workers stayed in the receiving country and a perma-nent immigrant population started to evolve in all Western European countries. In the 1970s the "second generation" issue also emerged around those children of immigrant ancestry who were born in Western Europe but were, in many ways, treated as foreigners because of their appearance or cultural characteristics.

Given the circumstances described above, a change of perspective became necessary. While the general Western European approach to migration was predominantly economic (developmental), it adopted a societal (integrationist) tone in the 1970s and 1980s. Originally, post-colonial immigration was treated within an "assimilationist" framework, while guest workers faced "differential exclusion." (Schierup et al., 2006, pp. 41-42) That is, workers from the ex-colonies were perceived as culturally non-different, while guest workers were implicitly excluded from the spheres of society that were not directly related to their work. These approaches became unsustainable and gave rise to multiculturalism, an ideological project that translated into public policies that aimed to accept immigrant groups and grant them equal social and cultural rights. (Kymlicka, 1995) Countries such as Sweden and the Netherlands adopted a multicultural immigration policy (in 1975 and 1983 respectively), and the United Kingdom also moved in this direction. France and Germany, however, rejected the multicultural model and kept to a social and cultural integrationist perspective. (Schierup et al., 2006)

Western European governments stopped recruiting foreign labor as a consequence of the 1973 oil crisis and, to some extent, tried to send migrants and guest workers back to their countries of origin, with very little success. From this point on a third (security) perspective was added to the migration issue with the above-mentioned concerns on sovereignty and border control. This perspective had already emerged in the 1970s, but it became predomi-nant only with the growing instability of the economic foundations of the Western European welfare regimes, which nonetheless continued to receive immigrants owing to ongoing family reunifications.

Following the fall of the Berlin Wall and the collapse of the Eastern Bloc, the European political scene changed radically. A wave of East-West migration emerged but, contrary to expectations, it did not immediately become a mass phenomenon. It was only in the early 2000s, given the poor economic performance of many Eastern European countries and the easing of travel restrictions, that significant Eastern European migrant communities appeared in Western European countries. (Castles & Miller, 2009)

Another, equally or more important feature of the 1990s, was that immigration flows to Western Europe became global and detached from previous historical ties. The neoliberal economic model became prevalent in the majority of the world's countries, and free trade and foreign investment contributed to the "uprooting of people," i.e. global competition broke the backbone of local economies in many developing countries, unemployment rates skyrocketed, and many people saw migration as the only way out of misery. (Sassen, 2006, p. 600) In the meantime, immigration legislation became stricter in the United States (and extremely strict after the 9/11 attacks in 2001), thus Europe emerged as a destination for migrants, especially South Americans and Southeast Asians, who traditionally had never arrived there in large numbers. Most of these migrants remained in big cities – hence Sassen's concept of "global cities" – and through subsequent waves of "amnesties" gained legal residence, especially in Spain and Italy. (Sassen, 2006, p. 604)

Currently, Europe hosts a migrant population of approximately 73 million people, of which 45 million live in EU-15 countries. These numbers refer to the population living in a country other than its country of citizenship, for more than one year (see detailed explanation below). Second- and third-generation migrants are left out of this figure, while intra-European migrants are included. (See Annex 2) One might assume that the free movement of workers, a fundamental principle enshrined in Article 45 of the Treaty on the Functioning of the European Union (TFEU), makes it meaningless to include European Union (EU) citizens in immigration statistics, but the reality shows that, especially in the case of Eastern Europeans in Western Europe, their socioeconomic status is practically the same as that of non-European immigrants. On the other hand, second- and third-generation migrants who hold citizenship in their Western European country of birth, show a socioeconomic status similar to their peers of non-immigrant ancestry who have an educational attainment similar to theirs. Nonetheless, differences can be observed on two extremely controversial issues: religious fundamentalism and racism/xenophobia. (Castles & Miller, 2009)

Radical Islam and welfare xenophobia

Radical Islam is the most commonly noted "threat" associated with migration in Western Europe. While there had already been hostilities before, it was after the 9/11 New York attacks that an overall Muslim threat became part of the global and the European discourse. In the post-9/11 years, two major terrorist attacks occurred in Europe that were carried out by second-generation immigrant Muslim fundamentalists: the 2004 Madrid and 2005 London bombings that killed 191 and 52 people respectively. Other well-known incidents include urban riots such as those in Paris in 2005, in London in 2011 or in Malmö in 2013, public outcry due to the infamous Muhammad caricatures published in the *Danish Jyllands-Posten* newspaper, and several, politically motivated crimes, most notably the assassination of Dutch politician Pim Fortuyn in 2002. Terrorist attacks in Russia, such as the 2004 Beslan hostage crisis, although carried out by Muslims (Chechens) do not belong to this line of events, as the attackers were not immigrants but autochthon nationals of a separatist region.

These acts of violence served as a base for a wave of racism/xenophobia, as they triggered a sense of insecurity among different groups in Western European societies. Meer and

Noorani found many similarities between pre-Second World War anti-Semitism and current anti-Muslim sentiment or Islamophobia. (Meer & Noorani, 2008) Many practices of orientalism in a Saidian sense can be found in current anti-Muslim discourses that resemble the classical anti-Semitic stereotypes: the filthy, sexually repressed, aggressive oriental Other, willing to take over the free West and defy its Enlightenment values. (See Said, 1977) Naturally there are many differences as well, but the parallelisms show that a discourse of this kind tells more about those who pronounce it than about its subjects.

Who pronounces and who shares the racist/xenophobic discourse? Investigating the sociological composition of far-right parties and anti-immigrant xenophobia in Europe, Betz arrived at the conclusion, long before 9/11, that in many ways it is the general resentment against the political class that gets channeled towards immigrants. (Betz, 1993) Working class voters in direct contact (and competition) with immigrants are possible targets of anti-immigrant political parties, but so also are entrepreneurial or self-employed middle class citizens who are against the state redistribution that supposedly favors the immigrants. It is true that welfare states in Western Europe had been quite generous to immigrants before the 2008 crisis – however, this kind of welfare chauvinism became ethnicized regardless of the actual proportion of immigrants (or people of immigrant background) who were net beneficiaries of social welfare transfers. Following regional studies' concept of "welfare nationalism" (McEwen, 2002) in wealthy Northwest European countries/regions, a sort of "welfare xenophobia" can be detected against immigrants in those same countries who are increasingly perceived as a threat to high living and welfare standards. This sort of welfare xenophobia has appeared and become increasingly popular among the precarious worker and self-employed segments of Western European societies.

On the other hand, the second generation's double-faced integration, and the glass ceiling they have been facing, has fed back into a fundamentalism which is, in many ways, a response to the low social status and constant exclusion they face. Many integrative policy attempts have sought to address this vicious circle. Curiously, these integration measures might also pour fuel on the fire: Vertovec suggests that positive discrimination and the increasing presence of migrant (Muslim or other) people in national or local governments and in the media may deepen the sense of being excluded among the disadvantaged groups of the majority society. (Vertovec, 2002) The anger then gets channeled against a non-specified "immigration" issue, even if it is against the second generation (already born in Western Europe) and not against actual migrants, that the discourse is pronounced.

Finally, the confusion between migrants and refugees also needs to be mentioned. As a UN Refugee Agency (UNHCR) study puts it, the line between the two groups, migrants and refugees, is blurry in the public mind, but the main concern is that it is so also in the policies of many states and local governments. (Feller, 2004) Nevertheless, "modern migratory patterns can make it sometimes difficult to distinguish between the various groups on the move. Population flows are rarely homogenous, but very often of a mixed character. Refugees are increasingly part of movements including both forced and voluntary departures." (Ibid., p. 2) While this is certainly the case, it must be mentioned that the international legal background of the two groups is very different, and so are the responsibilities of the state in cases of international protection and of simple labor migration. The former are based on the United Nations' *Convention relating to the Status of Refugees* (1951, Protocol in 1967) ratified by 146 countries, while for the latter, the United Nations' *Convention on the Protection of the Rights of All Migrant Workers and Members of Their Families* (signed 1990) is ratified by only 47, none of which a main country of destination for migration. Anti-immigration parties also find this confusion a good basis for welfare xenophobia, presenting questionable data on government spending on refugees as if it were relevant for all of the migrant population. Separation of these two issues in public discourse is certainly a central challenge for arriving at a clearer picture on migrants.

Table 1 summarizes the perception of, and public discourse on, social groups as "migrants" in Western Europe.

Table 1. Perception of social groups as "migrants" in Western Europe

	Country of birth of (1st generation) migrant				
1st generation	Born in an EU-15 country	Born in an EU-13 country	Born outside the EU but gained citizenship of an EU country	Born outside the EU and did not gain citizenship of an EU country	
2nd (3rd etc) generations	Their children and grandchildren (EU citizens)	Their children and grandchildren (EU citizens)	Their children and grandchildren (EU citizens)	Their children and grandchildren (EU citizens)	Their children and grandchildren (not EU citizens)

▬▬ Migrants
▬▬ Third country nationals
▬▬ Migrants and third country nationals
▭▭ Commonly referred to as migrants

Source: own compilation.

Migrants in Europe: beliefs and facts

But who is a migrant anyway? Definition problems come up as soon as we try to quantify the immigrant population. In the most used definition, that of the United Nations' *Recommendations on Statistics of International Migration, Rev. 1* (United Nations, 1998), a migrant is defined as "[a] person who moves to a country other than that of his or her usual residence for a period of at least a year (12 months), so that the country of destination effectively becomes his or her new country of usual residence," where "usual residence" is further defined as "the place at which the person has lived continuously for most of the last 12 months (…) not including temporary absences for holidays or work assignments, or intends to live for at least six months (…)." (Cited in Poulain & Herm, 2010, p. 6.) This definition is also echoed by Regulation (EC) No 862/2007 of the European Parliament and of the Council. (European Commission, 2007) In other words, if a person has lived for more than half of the previous year in a place which is not its country of citizenship, he or she is counted as a migrant.

There are several problems with this definition. First, this is by no means an official definition: even in the EU, definitions may vary as, for example, according to Germany's definition, any foreigner is counted as an immigrant in Germany after three months of continuous residence. Second, the acquis communautaire, as set out in the European directive on the right of citizens of the Union and their family members to move and reside freely within the territory of the Member States, makes it extremely difficult to track intra-EU population flows. (European Commission, 2003) Third, in connection with the right of free movement of persons, intra-EU migration is by no means definitive and it is not necessarily accompanied by a will towards assimilation. On the contrary, intra-EU migration tends to be temporary and circular.

As mentioned before, citizens of the European Union who live in another member state are not migrants in a legal sense, yet the socio-political reality of EU citizens in other EU countries (such as Romanians in Spain or Poles in the UK) reflects that they are perceived, treated and employed as immigrants and not as citizens of the same polity. The Eastern borders of Europe have always been a subject of heated debate (see Wolff, 1994; Bakic-Hayden, 1995; Böröcz & Sarkar, 2005, among others), leaving many countries in the "grey zone" that in Western European minds may or may not belong to Europe. This ranges from Hungary through Ukraine to Turkey, constituting an "East-West Slope." (Melegh, 2006)

Contrary to the popular anti-immigrant imagery in Western Europe that depicts immigrants as racially different and coming from another continent, most migrants within the 46 countries of the extended European area[1] stem from this in-between zone, cut in half by the EU's current borders. Using the United Nations immigrant definition detailed above and the World Bank's data for 2010, I have compiled a list of the top five immigrant groups (according to the country of birth) in each European country.[2] (See Annex 1) In many ways, these figures are more relevant than the aggregate data of a given nationality living in European countries other than their country of origin, as migration policies are still made, to a large extent, at the national level. It also needs to be noted that immigrant stocks according to the country of birth are larger than stocks according to citizenship, as migrants tend to acquire citizenship over time. Many "historical" communities are thus reflected in the following data, such as the Portuguese who emigrated in the 1960s and 1970s and in the meantime became French, German, Swiss etc. citizens.

In the Top 5 lists of immigrant groups in Europe, EU-15 (pre-enlargement) countries' natives appear in 27 cases, including all EU-15 countries with the exception of Italy and Greece. That is to say, among the main immigrant groups in Western Europe, a Western European nationality appears in 13 out of 15 cases. Nonetheless, the British in Spain, the Finnish in Sweden, or the Germans in Austria are not the typical subjects of the "immigration debate." The largest group of immigrants in Western European (EU-15) countries are EU-15 in six cases, Eastern European EU-members (EU-13) in three cases, Turkish in three cases and non-European in only three cases.

In the Eastern and Southeastern half of Europe that joined the EU through the enlargements of 2004, 2007 and 2013 (EU-13), the largest group of immigrants comes from EU-15

---

1   This analysis does not include Serbia, Kosovo and Montenegro because of the lack of consistent statistical time series caused by border changes.

2   The "wider Europe" region in this chapter stands for EU and (European Free Trade Association) EFTA countries, Balkan countries, Turkey and the ex-Soviet countries except for the five Central Asian states. "EU-15" refers to the countries which entered the EU before 2004, "EU-13" to those that entered in or after 2004. "Other European" is used for the remaining countries in the "wider Europe" region except for Turkey, which is treated separately due to its large share in East-West migratory flows.

countries in two cases (notably, the British in Cyprus and Malta), from EU-13 countries in three cases, from other European countries in seven cases, and from Turkey in one case. No non-European nationality figures as the most populous immigrant group in any EU-13 country.

Finally, a completely different migration system exists in the former Soviet area, with Russia and Ukraine at its core. The wider Europe is a conglomerate of a bigger and a smaller migration system, with Western Europe and Russia as the focal points. The borders of the two run somewhat to the East of the borders of the former Soviet Union, dividing countries such as Moldova that generate both West- and Russia-bound emigration. Also, counter-directional movements can be observed, as Russians and Western Europeans also emigrate. It is a curious fact that there are more UK-born people living abroad in the world than Turkey-born, however, one doesn't usually think of the British as a typical nation of emigrants.

Going back to our starting point, it must be said that perceptions of migration as an inward flow of masses of non-European population are completely wrong. The top 5 immigrant groups in the 46 countries analyzed add up to 230, out of which only 35 are from a non-European group (and another nine from Turkey). Out of these 35 occurrences, four (United States, Canada, Australia) belong to non-European countries of the Organisation for Economic Co-operation and Development (OECD), eight to countries of the Maghreb, ten to former colonies of the given European country (excluding the Maghreb) and 13 to other non-European countries.

Finally, the migratory balance of the observed 46 countries is relevant to the issue and shows that, out of these, 24 are net migrant-receiving and 22 are net migrant-sending. (See Annex 2) Thus, when we talk about migration in the wider Europe, we talk about a phenomenon that affects half of the continent in one way, and the other half, in another.

Map 1. Migratory balance in the countries of the wider Europe

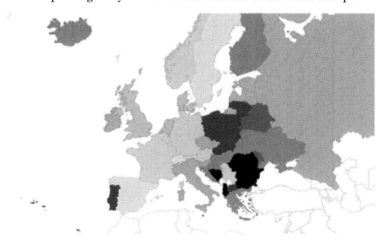

Source: own compilation, based on data from the World Bank (2010).

Challenge or opportunity? Theoretical notions

Based on the East-West split described above, the question of whether migration is a challenge or an opportunity for countries of the wider Europe must be formed in such a way as to entail challenges and opportunities for both sides. Migration theories are usually conceptualized from a clear economic/materialist standpoint. Following de Haas' overview of how migration theories deal with the issue of development, it can be stated that they regard migration as the establishing process of a spatial-economic equilibrium, even if it is "a strongly patterned process because people's individual choices are constrained by structural factors such as social stratification, market access, power inequalities as well as cultural repertoires affecting preferences." (de Haas, 2010, p. 5) These "distorting" patterns that hinder the equilibrium are actually so relevant that the neoclassical theory in itself cannot explain the direction, volume and composition of the specific migratory processes. The New Economy of Labor Migration takes a step forward in this respect, placing the household as the unit in focus, instead of the individual, making it a useful framework to understand the motivations of guest workers and debt migrants who are not seeking individual benefits but have to provide money for their families. Other theories, such as cumulative causation theory or network theory, put an emphasis on migrants using their personal networks to choose their destination (that may or may not be the best choice in formal cost-benefit terms), while world systems theory focuses on the historical-geographical dependent relations between migrant-sending and migrant-receiving countries. (Massey et al., 1993)

Most migration theories nonetheless operate on a micro level of analysis. When it comes to the balance on a national level, i.e. whether migration is a challenge or an opportunity for a given country, it becomes clear that national utility regarding migration is not the sum of the individual migrants' utility: migration also affects those who do not migrate. The following table presents a macro-level overview of the challenges and opportunities in migrant-sending and migrant-receiving countries, organized according to the principal approach the question is normally conceived from: development, integration, or security. Table 2 thus summarizes a wide range of statements (see references in the subsequent two chapters) that are shared by certain circles of migration researchers and that might be valid in certain particular settings. No country displays *all* elements listed here: however, the main features of most individual local designs are included in this table.

Table 2. Opportunities versus challenges in migrant-sending and migrant-receiving countries

		Migrant-receiving country	Migrant-sending country
Opportunities	Development approach	• Extra human capital and contribution to gross domestic product (brain gain) • Contribution to the social welfare system (migrant workers) • Increasing supply of labor in the DDD (dirty, dangerous, degrading) sector • Consumption of local goods by migrants • Cheaper products for the local poor	• Financial and social remittances • Decreasing unemployment • Growing competitiveness of the education system and student performance • Growth of exports due to diaspora demand
	Integration approach	• Cultural diversity as a source for innovation (e.g. ethnic niches) • Demonstration effect on migrant-sending countries (international prestige)	• Establishment of transnational diaspora networks and advocacy groups • Mobility channel and/or empowerment for the socially marginalized groups • Favorable change in gender relations
	Security approach		• Ensuring human rights and/or preventing humanitarian crisis
Challenges	Development approach	• Wage decreases and loss of employment for the non-migrants with "migrant jobs" • Pressure on the social welfare system (in connection with refugee and family reunification issues) • Deskilling, immigrant brain waste	• Loss of public money invested in education (brain drain) • Remittance dependency (financial, social) and lack of innovation • Lack of professionals in the skilled areas affected by emigration • Decreasing total fertility rate • Pressure on the social welfare system (lower share of taxpayers)
	Integration approach	• Marginalization of immigrants in economic and social terms • Fundamentalism and xenophobia	• Disarticulation of migrant-sending societies • Political passivity due to the "exit option"
	Security approach	• Threat of terrorism • Spread of epidemics Criminality	

Source: own compilation.

Opportunities for migrant-sending and migrant-receiving countries

The most important benefit of migration for the migrant-receiving country is that it receives a (generally) young adult population whose healthcare and education costs have been paid for by another country, resulting in a net transfer of human capital. Immigrants, besides making the migrant-receiving country's economy more dynamic through their work and consumption, also have positive structural effects on the economy. They fill in the gaps in the labor market shunned by the natives given the DDD (dirty, dangerous, degrading) nature of many of these jobs, while unemployment decreases in the migrant-sending country. Highly skilled migrants may enjoy better professional opportunities in the receiving country and, again, a more competitive wage, a part of which can be translated as remittances or even investment. (Borjas, 2006)

Furthermore, there are benefits that do not stem from the differences in wages but from the cultural background, most importantly in terms of entrepreneurial culture. Scholars who represent the integration approach emphasize that cultural diversity is a value in itself, both in societal and economic terms. Multiculturalism, in the sense of the public policies described above, has favored the formation of ethnic enterprises, ranging from Chinese retail stores to Turkish fast food restaurants. The term "ethnic enterprises" was coined by Ivan Light in the 1970s, drawing on Edna Bonacich's "middleman minorities" theory. (Light, 1972; Bonacich, 1973) According to Zhou, a larger concept, "ethnic economies," is more adequate, and in turn can refer to either "ethnic enclave economies" where the entrepreneurs have a clientele constituted by their co-ethnics, or to "middleman minorities" proper, who serve a larger, majority (or other minority) spectrum of customers. (Zhou, 2004) Ethnic enterprises therefore have the advantage of providing cheaper goods for the local population as they have privileged access to distribution chains connecting their countries of origin and destination. This is especially the case with the Chinese, Vietnamese and Indian diasporas, many of whose members enjoy a stable livelihood based on these types of commercial activities.

For the migrant-sending countries, the most important opportunity entailed by migration is that migrants can work for a better wage. Most migratory movements are primarily economy-driven, and the surplus money that stems from the difference in wages between the two countries is seen by the migrant as the net benefit of migration. Saved money is sent back home as remittances, a flow of private money transfers that in 2012 exceeded USD 500 billion worldwide. Regarding Europe, in 2009 USD 24.5 billion were taken out of and USD 35.4 billion sent in to the countries of the wider Europe region from elsewhere. (*Migration and Remittances Factbook*, 2011, p. 26) This is an interesting figure because generally it is thought that in the European context, remittances are money transfers that go from Europe to the developing countries. This might be the case in some countries, however, as has been explained above, the overwhelming majority of migrants in Europe are Europeans. Even wealthy countries such as France and the United Kingdom are net remittance receivers, the former sending USD 5.2 billion and receiving USD 15.9 billion, the latter USD 3.7 billion and 7.4 billion respectively. In other cases the balance is negative, but not dramatically so: USD 15.9 billion went out of and USD 11.6 billion were sent in to Germany as remittances in 2009. (*Migration and Remittances Factbook*, 2011, pp. 13-15)

In the migrant-sending country, family members can live off the remittances. These amount to a private salary, and as such can be spent as a locally earned salary would be: either on non-durable and durable consumer goods, or in savings for investment. In any case, this means that the economy receives an amount of foreign currency that otherwise would not have been generated and directed to the migrant-sending country. As the migrant's family members spend the money, they then generate additional economic activity, a phenomenon known as the multiplier effect. Remittances are also more resistant to crisis than foreign direct investment (FDI), as their main driving force is not economic rationale but solidarity.

Migrant entrepreneurs can "make it" and become owners of large sums of money that can affect positively their sending country in several ways. According to Manuel Orozco's "5 T-model" it is trade, transportation, telecommunication, transfer of remittances and tourism between the migrant-sending and the migrant-receiving country that yields business opportunities for the ethnic entrepreneur, and a development potential for the migrant-sending country. (Orozco, 2005)

The weaving of transnational networks can also empower women, ethnic, religious or sexual minorities, or other marginalized or dissident social groups in the migrant-sending country who can either become a migrant and thus enhance their human capabilities, or benefit from "social remittances." This term, coined by Peggy Levitt, comprises "normative structures, ideas, values, and beliefs," "systems of practice" and "social capital." (Levitt, 2001) Originally the author was referring to these assets on the individual level, showing the ideal type of successful (rich) returning migrants who bring from the migrant-receiving country a new, fresh look on the problems of their home country. Although not every belief and social practice in the migrant-receiving countries is undoubtedly positive, it can be said that richer societies generally cherish self-realization values, in contrast to poorer societies based on survival values (Inglehart & Baker, 2000), therefore the impact of migrants can help the economic-organizational structure of these societies to move towards the former given the adequate economic conditions. However, this is not always the case: returning migrants' new ideas and values often face rejection in the country of origin, especially from those members of the society who enjoy privileges that these "new" ideas and values would challenge.

Finally, from a security studies viewpoint, migration as an exit (refugee) option can help ensure human rights and/or prevent humanitarian crises. In cases of natural disasters, wars or persecution of given groups of society, leaving the country can actually save people's lives. The refugee condition, presented above, has blurry borders, and is in many cases difficult to separate from economic motivations. Less abrupt motivations for leaving also include climate change, which many forecasts see as one of the key drivers of migration in the future. (Brown, 2008) The security perspective thus recognizes the positive effects of migration on the sending countries, but conceives of no such effects for the receiving country, where migration is seen as an overall challenge, burden or threat.

Challenges for the migrant-sending and the migrant-receiving country

The flip side of the migratory process is the major developmental challenge resulting from migrants' willingness to accept lower wages and worse working conditions than natives. This causes an overall lowering of salaries in the types of jobs that are normally taken by immigrants. As migration is very much a network-dependent issue, migrants of a given ethnicity may "crowd out" natives (and competing immigrant groups) from certain occupational areas, such as Moldovans in Italy in the area of domestic healthcare service. In a study of what happens to natives who lose their jobs because of competition with immigrants, Cattaneo et al. found that on the macro level the native population moves towards an upper segment of the labor market through personal networks or subsidized training courses. (Cattaneo et al., 2013) In this respect, competition with immigrant workers pushes natives upwards which, if they succeed, might be seen as a win-win outcome. However, this is not always the case on the micro level. Ethnicization of lower-skilled jobs leads to segregation on the one hand,

and to frustration and/or failure on the other, for those natives who cannot re-invent their professional identity once they have been replaced in their original job by an immigrant. (Boubtane et al., 2011)

This can happen regardless of the fact that many migrants work in job areas for which they are overqualified. Not using existing skills and expertise is known as brain waste, and is a joint outcome of many factors ranging from qualifications unfamiliar to the employers and no local work experience, through lack of language proficiency, to simple racism. (Sumption, 2013) Some occupations also require licensing or registration, while in others a strong labor union can block immigrants' access to specific jobs. According to the United Kingdom's Labour Force Survey, for example, among migrants from Eastern Europe (EU-13) who work in the UK in elementary occupations, i.e. those that require no specific qualifications at all, 36% left full-time education at an age higher than 20 years (*Labour mobility*, 2009, p. 99), meaning that they possess high school, professional school or even university degrees. This is a lose-lose situation.

Moving a bit further from the economic problems migration can cause, we enter the realm of security studies. Primary security concerns rise from the challenge that migration poses to the idea of national sovereignty and border control. Along with fear of radical Islam and terrorism, the limited ability of a liberal state to control who is entering and staying on its territory is a root cause of anti-system extremism. From a sociological viewpoint, however, it is not the so-called illegal immigration (i.e. unauthorized entry or stay beyond the authorized length of visit) that causes problems, but the subsequent marginalization that an undocumented migrant may face. The ghettoization of immigrants, seen through xenophobic eyes as a proof of the immigrants' immanent inability to adapt to the migrant-receiving country's norms and values, is often a produce of marginalization due to legal and economic constraints. (Stolcke, 1995) A large number of problems may actually stem from a population that goes into hiding and does not seek contact with any "authority," not even the healthcare system, sometimes causing migrants to be branded as potential disease spreaders in public discourse. Criminality is also directly related to irregular migratory status, as people with no valid documents can only work in the shadow economy, sometimes trading illicit goods (drugs, weapons, human smuggling etc.).

Public policies have addressed the issue of irregular migration using two major approaches: regularization and deportation, both accompanied by the strengthening of border control. En masse regularizations for three million undocumented migrants took place in Southern Europe between 1997 and 2007. However, this practice was abruptly brought to an end following an outcry from other EU member states' governments and the unfolding of the financial crisis. (Brick, 2011, p. 4) Despite a bitter academic debate on its legal bases (see Paoletti, 2010), governments are finding the deportation option increasingly attractive. The United Kingdom, one of the European countries with the strictest rules for deportation, removed 41,482 people from its territory in 2011, paying an approximate GBP 11,000 for each repatriate (Blinder, 2012), making it an economically unsustainable measure against unauthorized stay. Putting human rights issues aside and deporting irregular migrants without any trial would be the cheap solution but it is, fortunately, not an option in a democracy.

Turning the focus to migrant-sending countries, the key issue to handle is the loss of human capital. Education, housing, food, clothes etc. provided to children in the first years of their life are difficult to measure in exact financial terms, but it is evident that the family and the state spend money on bringing up children that then do not contribute to either the family's or the state's budget. Emigration is, nonetheless, tolerated by society, and prospective migrants hold very high expectations about "making it" abroad. This is mainly because migrant-sending societies have a distorted view of migrant-receiving countries, first because the United States and Western Europe are presented in the media as the land of plenty, where streets are paved with gold, and second because migrants themselves confirm this myth when in contact with non-migrant co-nationals in order to avoid facing cognitive dissonance. (Glick Schiller & Fouron, 2001)

Remittances, although the principal gain from migration, do not always benefit the local economy. In many cases, they are spent under conditions of dependency that, both as an economic and a psychological condition, lead the members of the migrant-sending household to spend the remittances on consumer goods made in the migrant-receiving country. This is certainly the case in societies where migration has a strong symbolic context, as in the Eastern Europe – Western Europe relation. Defining whether remittances are spent on locally produced goods – and consequently whether they have an important spillover effect – is a function of the local economy's structure. In many migrant-sending countries, transnational companies possess the majority of the consumer goods' market, eventually taking back the profit to the migrant-receiving country. (Sørensen, 2004)

Besides loss of human capital (brain drain), remittance dependency and personal hardships, emigration leads to a loss of professionals in key skill areas, which further burdens the development of the migrant-sending country. Other features include political passivity due to the easy "exit option," and the decreasing of the total fertility rate, as a large share of migrants are young adults who need to postpone their child-bearing or, if they settle down in the receiving country, raise their children there, further worsening the age structure of the migrant-sending country. Societies can, therefore, experience many disarticulating tendencies that appear when emigration is on the rise. (Delgado et al., 2009)

The devil is in the details: an uneasy balance

Recapitulating what has been said on the challenges and opportunities of migration, two points need to be made. First, as has been shown, migration in Europe is very much an intra-continental issue, even if this appears differently in public discourse. Second, it entails a lengthy menu of challenges and opportunities for both migrant-sending and migrant-receiving countries, from which very different, either healthy or harmful diets can be compiled. What do long-term development patterns suggest? Basically, it is the demographic and labor market variables that matter, however, migration policies can also modify the picture, for better or worse.

As has been stated at the very beginning of the present chapter, Europe was a net migrant-sending area until the 1960s when colonial empires were dismantled, political stability was reached and the post-Second World War economic miracle (*Les Trente Glorieuses* in France, *Wirtschaftswunder* in Germany) created so many jobs that an intense demand for unskilled labor appeared in Western Europe. The net migration rate turned positive and it was basically labor-driven, contributing to the economic boom. Although on a much humbler level, Southern European countries, especially Italy and Spain, had similar labor market processes in the 1990s and the first half of the 2000s, creating a second wave of labor immigration. (Arango, 2013) Better-off Eastern European countries, although many scholars expected that with time they would also become significant migrant-receiving countries, never experienced such large-scale immigration.

The common features of the 1960s and 1970s in Western Europe and the 1990s and 2000s in Southern Europe is that labor markets were expanding and immigration, especially of low-skilled personnel, was very much in demand. As described by the dual labor market theory of migration (Massey et al., 1993), native populations moved towards stable and white-collar jobs while immigrants occupied the lower and more precarious segment of the labor market. Migration was seen, both by natives and immigrants, as a developmentally positive process. On the side of the migrant-sending countries, a major demographic transition was unfolding, with a drop in deaths and rise in live births creating a young, unemployed population surplus. Additionally, the migrant-sending countries (the Mediterranean region in the 1960s and 1970s, Yugoslavia, Turkey, the Maghreb and, to a lesser extent, Sub-Saharan Africa, Latin America and South Asia in the 1990s and 2000s) reached an economic welfare level that enabled people to cover the costs of migration, as conceptualized by the "migration hump" theory. (Martin & Taylor, 1996)

While in these two temporal and spatial settings the overall developmental effects of migration could be seen as positive for both the migrant-sending and the migrant-receiving countries, it is not that evident in other cases. Western Europe's economic growth slowed down, second- and third-generation migrants (or, better, Western European citizens of migrant ancestry) grew up and became marginalized, productive industries gradually moved to non-European countries and the need for unskilled labor dropped dramatically. The labor market has concentrated around technology- and knowledge-intensive industries and services. At the same time, population ageing has become a crucial issue and the role of healthcare has grown in an unprecedented way. As a consequence, low-skilled labor migration has gradually shifted from being the fuel of economic growth to being a scapegoat for economic stagnation and loss of working-class jobs. The majority of public opinion in Western Europe understands migration (including and/or deliberately confusing with the second-generation and the refugee issues) as more of a challenge than an opportunity in economic terms. (Eurobarometer, 2010, pp. 51-60)

However, governments are very much aware that the European economy needs skilled immigrants in a broad range of occupational areas, listed in publications such as those of the European Centre for the Development of Vocational Training (CEDEFOP) and reflected in public policy instruments such as the Blue Card (see below). (CEDEFOP, 2012) Public opinion also shares this notion, and highly skilled professionals' migration to Europe is seen as a development opportunity. Again, a strange case of welfare xenophobia seems to be at play: curiously, the 2010 Eurobarometer survey shows that Western European respondents, who have experience with immigrants working in economically important areas, differentiate between migrant and migrant according to the (subjective) utility of the work they do, as opposed to respondents from Eastern Europe where immigrant populations are smaller and where the majority of the respondents do not want immigrants at all, regardless of their skills.

Having mentioned Eastern Europe, it must also be said that this region has witnessed a dramatic shrinking of the labor market following the transition to democracy, due to the collapse of the socialist systems of production and to privatization under neoliberal premises. This led to several waves of migration towards Western Europe, benefiting from the gradual opening of the EU member states' labor markets from 2004 onwards. However, these are also ageing societies with a net population decrease and relatively high government spending, as opposed to other sources of immigration to Western Europe. (Gödri et al., 2014) Thus, negative consequences of emigration can be very severe in this region regarding demography, skilled labor supply and government budget, although several different "historical development patterns" can be outlined. Countries such as Slovenia may become migrant-receiving countries, while others such as Romania or Serbia are very much likely to remain migrant-sending. Some of the countries have a very delicate balance of immigration and emigration, such as Hungary and Slovakia. (Melegh, 2012) It can be said, therefore, that migration also poses several challenges to the migrant-sending half of Europe.

Brain drain, care drain and lack of professionals in the skill areas exposed to emigration are of concern all over the globe. The EU is not the only target for global migration: the United States, Canada, the Gulf States, Australia or Singapore are also popular destinations for skilled migrants. There is an increasingly sharpening global competition for the best and brightest, in which the EU holds a good position, which, on the other hand, implies important responsibilities. If many skilled migrants arrived to Western Europe, it would certainly turn migration into an opportunity and not a challenge for that geographical area, but for the migrant-sending countries in Eastern Europe, the Maghreb or Sub-Saharan Africa it would be exactly the opposite. By fostering circular migration, i.e. providing the opportunity for professionals to move back and forth between the migrant-sending and migrant-receiving countries, a more favorable development outcome could be realized on the global level. (Betts & Cerna, 2011)

Policy making on a contested issue

According to the categorization by Zincone and Caponio, research on migration in Europe has undergone several stages, of which research on policies is the most recent. (Zincone and Caponio, 2006, p. 269) The authors distinguish between the phases of research on 1. migration's demography and spatiality, 2. migrants' economic and social behavior, 3. migrants' social and political integration and 4. migration policies and their institutional background. This means that the corpus of migration literature has not, until very recently, dealt with the issue of how migration is and should be managed. Policy making has been, therefore, quite spontaneous and driven by impressions rather than long-term goals and evidence.

Policy making related to migration is relevant on three levels of action: local, national and European. Local governance is generally the most straightforward: they have immigrants to deal with, or emigrants to keep connected somehow to their hometown. Locally conceived immigrant integration policies tend to be less ideologically-driven than those that are pronounced by political parties on a national level. However, local governments have a very limited effect on migratory flows that are, by nature, moved by transnational factors. National-level governance is powerful in shaping the legal framework of migration control, but it is challenged from below by voters' opinion on the migration issue (which is, according to the polls cited, not very favorable to immigration, and easily blames the government if emigration is on the rise) and, from above, by transnational processes that can to some extent affect the overall direction of migration flows without being able to change it. Finally, on the European level, while the scope of action is adequate, the EU lacks the instruments to harmonize member states' migration policies and force them to concrete action. It does, however, have important tools for influencing the other two levels, which Zincone and Caponio see as the opportunity for a nascent multilevel governance approach for the migratory processes. Given the approach of the present chapter, I will enter into details only as far as policy making on the European level is concerned.

The most comprehensive document to date, the *Communication from the Commission regarding The Global Approach to Migration and Mobility* (GAMM) – organizes the existing migration-related measures and tools in a logical framework. It establishes four, "equally important pillars: 1. organising and facilitating legal migration and mobility; 2. preventing and reducing irregular migration and trafficking in human beings; 3. promoting international protection and enhancing the external dimension of asylum policy; 4. maximising the development impact of migration and mobility." (European Commission, 2011, p. 7) The first pillar includes measures such as the Blue Card Directive (on highly skilled workers), the Single Permit Directive (establishing a single procedure for immigration permits), the Professional Qualifications Directive (that helps to recognize migrants' qualifications) and several other directives mainly on labor and study migration. The second gathers the FRONTEX agency and other border control bodies. In the third, regional protection programs are the main elements that aim at refugee reception in the region of origin. The fourth puts forward recommendations and partnership proposals to combat brain drain and maximize the development impact of remittances.

GAMM understands migration as the act of entering the European Union from the territory of a third country, and in this respect the four pillars are relevant and adequate. However, as has been shown in this chapter, migration is much more than that. It is also intra-EU mobility that does not, legally, count as migration but, sociologically, does. Following an EU logic, EU citizens in another EU country do not count as migrants, not even when it comes to specific programs for marginalized social groups financed by the European Social Fund. A good example of what this means in practice is migrant non-government organization funding in Portugal, where associations representing Moldovan immigrants are entitled to receive European Social Fund (ESF) subsidies, while those representing Romanians are not, although these national groups share the same social situation in Portugal. (Sardinha, 2009) GAMM also disregards the fact that EU citizens actually emigrate from Europe, heading to North and South America, East Asia or elsewhere. Foreign policy instruments such as the EU-Africa Strategic Partnership on Migration or the Prague Process are exclusively focused on immigration to Europe.

Furthermore, the EU has a double-faced approach to migratory links with developing countries. Despite GAMM's emphasis that migration is a tool for development – a point further stressed by the communication of the European Commission on *Maximising the Development Impact of Migration*, which states that "migration and mobility must be recognised as 'enabling factors' for development" (European Commission, 2013, p. 4) – this is the weakest pillar with no unified instruments such as the Blue Card or FRONTEX. It is very telling that the first pillar (for attracting skilled labor to the EU) includes a large number of influential policy tools, while the fourth, with which it is in clear contradiction in view of the brain and care drain it might generate, does not have any.

To sum up, the EU's migration policy, as the European Commission itself, is made up of different national interests, evolving towards the line of least resistance. The Blue Card, although it also raised concerns, is a widely accepted instrument, and so is FRONTEX. On the other hand, the Commission does not seem to be taking any measures towards making EU member states ratify the United Nations Convention on the Protection of the Rights of All Migrant Workers and Members of Their Families. Additionally, the legal category of a single EU citizenship does not tackle the problem of inequality in wages and professional perspectives that fuel migration from the East to the West and that still remain crucial despite the many development projects funded by the European Regional Development Fund. Thus, what is understood as freedom of movement for workers from a Brussels perspective, might perfectly well be understood as brain drain in Eastern Hungary.

Conclusion

In a globalized world with an ever-increasing competition for human capital, the European Union is one of the most attractive regions of destination for highly skilled migrants. Key EU documents such as the Lisbon Strategy and the Europe 2020 Strategy envisage a competitive and knowledge-based economy for the Union, for which several steps have been taken on a migration policy level, such as the above-mentioned Blue Card and Single Permit instruments.

However, a central point of this chapter has been that what is true for Western Europe's "global cities" is not necessarily so for the whole "wider Europe" region. As has been demonstrated by the figures of Annexes 1 and 2, half of the continent is a net migrant-sending area sending labor migrants to the other, net migrant-receiving half. This is largely an East-to-West process, where "East" refers to the former Socialist bloc, regardless of the current EU membership of the given country. Thus, on an all-European level it is important to look in a balanced way at the migration issue, equally taking into account migrant-sending and migrant-receiving countries. (Annex 2)

A number of conceptual questions further arise over the definition of migrants. EU citizens in another EU country are not considered migrants in legal terms, however, in sociological terms they certainly are. Second- and third-generation migrants in Western Europe (that is, Western European countries' citizens with a migrant ancestry) are by no means migrants themselves, but are often treated as such in the political discourse. Finally, refugees are often confused with (labor) migrants. This conceptual blurriness can be very useful for extremist parties who find convenient scapegoats in the above-mentioned social groups, deliberately confusing the characteristics of different migrant categories.

Currently, various discourses exist on migration, of which this chapter has chosen to present the main elements of what can be dubbed the development approach. The aim of this approach is to answer the question also posed in the title, i.e. whether migration is a challenge or an opportunity for a country or a region. The analytical framework presented in Figure 1 has shown that no simple answer exists to this question, as there are abundant positive and negative factors for both migrant-sending and migrant-receiving countries. A comprehensive, multi-level governance approach is needed to enhance the positive factors and to reduce the negative ones. Parts of this approach can be found in the European Commission's *Global Approach to Migration and Mobility* document which does not, on the other hand, deal with many of the above-mentioned features. (European Commission, 2013)

A good path to follow should be reducing the opportunity losses that a migratory process entails. Fostering circular migration and fighting the situations of "brain waste" are certainly important steps to be taken. Also, as migrants are constructing transnational spaces through modern technology, their "presence" in their country of origin is palpable also while they are away. For migrant-sending countries it is crucial that emigrants remain connected to their sending communities.

Human mobility is one of the most crucial issues to tackle in the 21st century. The more win-win situations can be achieved on a local, national and regional level through public policies, the more likely it will be that migratory processes become development opportunities rather than development challenges.

Annexes

Annex 1. Top 5 immigrant nationalities in each country by country of birth, 2010 (World Bank estimate)

Albania		Andorra		Armenia	
TOTAL	89,106	TOTAL	55,847	TOTAL	324,184
Greece	80,778	Spain	34,925	Azerbaijan	164,483
Macedonia, FYR	6,457	Portugal	9,014	Georgia	75,792
Czech Republic	1,075	France	5,805	Russian Federation	32,993
Israel	100	United Kingdom	1,265	Iran, Islamic Rep.	18,154
Italy	73	Morocco	628	Syrian Arab Rep.	6,065

Austria		Azerbaijan		Belarus	
TOTAL	1,310 218	TOTAL	263,940	TOTAL	1,090,378
Germany	202,093	Russian Federation	50,007	Russian Federation	680,497
Bosnia and Herzegovina	162,362	Armenia	42,596	Poland	235,853
Turkey	160,698	Ukraine	10,234	Ukraine	141,266
Serbia	130,844	Georgia	5,258	Armenia	6,074
Poland	76,465	Other South	155,844	Lithuania	3,807

Belgium		Bosnia and Herzegovina		Bulgaria	
TOTAL	1,465 677	TOTAL	27,780	TOTAL	107,245
France	174,750	Croatia	9,734	Turkey	98,148
Morocco	172,682	Albania	63	Other South	9,097
Italy	129,769	Ukraine	50		
Netherlands	127,812	Slovenia	28		
Turkey	94,554	Other North	17,574		

Croatia		Cyprus		Czech Republic	
TOTAL	699,947	TOTAL	154,253	TOTAL	453,041
Bosnia and Herzegovina	532,528	United Kingdom	32,146	Slovak Republic	288,276
Slovenia	25,642	Greece	20,937	Ukraine	33,642
Macedonia, FYR	12,047	Georgia	13,497	Poland	24,958
Germany	9,618	Russian Fed.	11,484	Vietnam	14,788
Other South	103,432	Sri Lanka	8,723	Russian Federation	13,470

Denmark		Estonia		Finland	
TOTAL	483,714	TOTAL	182,464	TOTAL	225,646
Turkey	40,153	Russian Federation	137,860	Sweden	33,651
Germany	32,992	Ukraine	18,216	Estonia	18,637
Iraq	27,057	Belarus	10,765	Russian Federation	17,534
Poland	23,640	Latvia	3,129	Somalia	6,464
Bosnia and Herzegovina	22,977	Other South	9,736	Germany	5,893

France		Georgia		Germany	
TOTAL	6,684 842	TOTAL	167,269	TOTAL	10,758,061
Algeria	913,794	Russian Federation	109,968	Turkey	2,733,109
Morocco	840,985	Armenia	17,769	Italy	842,666
Portugal	762,411	Azerbaijan	7,819	Poland	613,768
Italy	450,394	Ukraine	7,447	Greece	470,350
Spain	364,177	Turkey	6,206	Croatia	359,367

Greece		Hungary		Iceland	
TOTAL	1,132 794	TOTAL	368,076	TOTAL	37,223
Albania	676,846	Romania	189,055	Denmark	5,026
Bulgaria	53,973	Germany	26,387	Poland	3,621
Romania	45,289	Austria	6,651	Sweden	3,408
Georgia	41,817	China	4,859	United States	3,071
Russian Federation	37,980	Other South	63,287	Germany	2,476

Ireland		Italy		Latvia	
TOTAL	898,630	TOTAL	4,463,413	TOTAL	335,022
United Kingdom	397,465	Romania	813,037	Russian Federation	203,920
Poland	93,330	Albania	522,647	Ukraine	33,090
United States	36,802	Morocco	475,783	Uzbekistan	22,872
Lithuania	36,754	China	203,519	Belarus	11,488
Nigeria	24,383	Ukraine	172,571	Kazakhstan	11,075

Liechtenstein		Lithuania		Luxembourg	
TOTAL	12,538	TOTAL	128,855	TOTAL	173,232
Switzerland	4,214	Russian Federation	60,302	Portugal	49,861
Austria	2,222	Belarus	35,502	France	22,494
Germany	1,253	Ukraine	12,692	Belgium	17,665
Italy	1,139	Latvia	5,274	Germany	15,365
Turkey	982	Kazakhstan	4,142	Italy	14,656

Macedonia, FYR		Malta		Moldova	
TOTAL	129,701	TOTAL	15,456	TOTAL	408,319
Albania	91,128	United Kingdom	5,129	Ukraine	189,906
Turkey	13,955	Australia	2,450	Russian Federation	147,802
Serbia	6,433	Canada	960	Bulgaria	42,871
Bosnia and Herzegovina	3,046	Italy	710	Belarus	2,631
Other South	15,138	Other North	4,231	Other South	25,109

Monaco		Netherlands		Norway	
TOTAL	23,572	TOTAL	1,752,869	TOTAL	485,444
France	9,298	Turkey	195,029	Sweden	47,908
Italy	5,827	Suriname	187,219	Denmark	28,732
United Kingdom	1,548	Morocco	167,355	United States	21,416
Belgium	716	Indonesia	146,854	Iraq	21,361
Other North	5,826	Germany	117,170	Pakistan	21,284

Poland		Portugal		Romania	
TOTAL	827,453	TOTAL	918,626	TOTAL	132,757
Ukraine	332,950	Angola	245,650	Moldova	39,091
Belarus	112,197	France	134,355	Bulgaria	19,752
Germany	104,710	Mozambique	107,190	Ukraine	13,890
Lithuania	85,057	Brazil	70,350	Russian Federation	7,760
Russian Federation	58,851	Cape Verde	63,403	Syrian Arab Rep.	7,346

Russian Federation		San Marino		Slovak Republic	
TOTAL	12,270 388	TOTAL	11,683	TOTAL	130,682
Ukraine	3,647 234	Italy	11,420	Czech Republic	67,801
Kazakhstan	2,648 315	Other North	263	Hungary	14,160
Belarus	958,719			Ukraine	8,353
Uzbekistan	940,539			Poland	4,555
Azerbaijan	866,843			Russian Federation	3,638

Slovenia		Spain		Sweden	
TOTAL	163,894	TOTAL	6,900,547	TOTAL	1,306,020
Bosnia and Herz.	82,669	Romania	810,471	Finland	189,535
Croatia	26,141	Morocco	778,451	Iraq	103,728
Macedonia, FYR	15,650	Ecuador	519,123	Poland	61,888
Other North	6,903	United Kingdom	411,074	Bosnia and Herz.	59,264
Other South	22,402	Colombia	375,710	Denmark	48,869

Switzerland		Turkey		Ukraine	
TOTAL	1,762 797	TOTAL	1,410,947	TOTAL	5,257,527
Italy	263,320	Bulgaria	538,686	Russian Federation	3,684,217
Germany	204,233	Germany	306,456	Belarus	276,070
Portugal	113,320	Greece	66,344	Kazakhstan	249,886
France	110,377	Macedonia, FYR	35,308	Uzbekistan	247,151
Spain	69,220	Netherlands	24,450	Moldova	168,370

United Kingdom		Total number of European emigrants in the world, top 5 countries		Total number of European emigrants in the world, by country group	
TOTAL	6,955 738	TOTAL	64,368,687	TOTAL	64,368,687
India	657,792	Russian Fed.	11,034,681	EU15	21,972,356
Poland	521,446	Ukraine	6,525,145	EU10	5,769,648
Pakistan	451,712	United K.	4,666,172	EU2+1	4,723,773
Ireland	422,569	Turkey	4,261,786	EFTA	640,380
Germany	299,753	Italy	3,480,280	Other European	31,262,531

Source: Own compilation based on World Bank (2010).

Annex 2. Immigrant stock in European countries and emigrant stock from the same countries (of birth)

	Emigrant stock	Immigrant stock	E/I ratio
Albania	1,438,451	89,106	16.14
Andorra	9,253	55,847	0.17
Armenia	870,458	324,184	2.69
Austria	597,639	1,310,218	0.46
Azerbaijan	1,433,513	263,940	5.43
Belarus	1,765,877	1,090,378	1.62
Belgium	454,522	1,465,677	0.31
Bosnia and Herzegovina	1,460,639	27,780	52.58
Bulgaria	1,201,191	107,245	11.20
Croatia	753,529	699,947	1.08
Cyprus	149,557	154,253	0.97
Czech Republic	369,737	453,041	0.82
Denmark	259,358	483,714	0.54
Estonia	169,213	182,464	0.93
Finland	329,269	225,646	1.46
France	1,738,006	6,684,842	0.26
Georgia	1,058,300	167,269	6.33
Germany	3,529,460	10,758,061	0.33
Greece	1,209,813	1,132,794	1.07
Hungary	462,418	368,076	1.26
Iceland	42,693	37,223	1.15
Ireland	736,889	898,630	0.82
Italy	3,480,280	4,463,413	0.78
Latvia	275,177	335,022	0.82
Liechtenstein	6,171	12,538	0.49
Lithuania	429,016	128,855	3.33
Luxembourg	57,787	173,232	0.33
Macedonia, FYR	447,138	129,701	3.45
Malta	107,412	15,456	6.95
Moldova	770,528	408,319	1.89
Monaco	18,533	23,572	0.79
Netherlands	992,913	1,752,869	0.57
Norway	183,936	485,444	0.38
Poland	3,155,509	827,453	3.81
Portugal	2,229,620	918,626	2.43
Romania	2,769,053	132,757	20.86
Russian Federation	11,034,681	12,270,388	0.90
San Marino	3,111	11,683	0.27
Slovak Republic	519,716	130,682	3.98
Slovenia	131,895	163,894	0.80
Spain	1,373,024	6,900,547	0.20
Sweden	317,605	1,306,020	0.24
Switzerland	407,581	1,762,797	0.23
Turkey	4,261,786	1,410,947	3.02
Ukraine	6,525,145	5,257,527	1.24
United Kingdom	4,666,172	6,955,738	0.67

No consistent time series:			
Kosovo			
Montenegro			
Serbia			

Source: Own compilation based on World Bank (2010).

Bibliography

Arango, J. (2013). *Exceptional in Europe? Spain's Experience with Immigration and Integration.* Washington DC: Migration Policy Institute.

Bakic-Hayden, M. (1995). Nesting Orientalisms: The Case of Former Yugoslavia. *Slavic Review.* 54(4), 917–931.

Betts, A., & Cerna, L. (2011). High-Skilled Labour Migration. In A. Betts, *Global Migration Governance* (pp. 60–77). Oxford: Oxford University Press.

Betz, H-G. (1993). The New Politics of Resentment. Radical Right-Wing Populist Parties in Western Europe. *Comparative Politics.* 25(4), 413–427.

Blinder, S. (2012). Deportations, Removals and Voluntary Departures from the UK. (Migration Observatory briefing). COMPAS, University of Oxford, UK. Retrieved from http://www.migrationobservatory.ox.ac.uk/briefings/deportations-removals-and-voluntary-departures-uk. Visited 14.08.2013.

Bonacich, E. (1973). A Theory of Middleman Minorities. *American Sociological Review.* 38(5), 583–594.

Borjas, G. (2006). The New Economics of Immigration: Affluent Americans Gain; Poor Americans Lose. In A. Messina & G. Lahav, *The Migration Reader. Exploring Politics and Policies* (pp. 318-328). London – Boulder: Lynne Rienner.

Böröcz, J., & Sarkar, M. (2005). What Is the EU? *International Sociology.* 20(2), 153–173.

Boubtane, E., Coulibaly, D., & Rault, Ch. (2011). Immigration, Unemployment and Growth in the Host Country: Bootstrap Panel Granger Causality. Analysis on OECD Countries. (IZA Discussion Paper No. 5853). Bonn: Institute for the Study of Labor (IZA). Retrieved from http://ftp.iza.org/dp5853.pdf. Visited 14.09.2013.

Brettel, C., & Hollifield, J. (2008). Migration Theory: Talking across Disciplines. In C. Brettel & J. Hollifield, *Migration Theory: Talking across Disciplines.* New York: Routledge.

Brick, K. (2011). *Regularizations in the European Union: The Contentious Policy Tool.* Washington, DC: Migration Policy Institute.

Brown, O. (2008). Migration and Climate Change. (IOM Migration Research Series No. 31). Geneva. International Organization for Migration. Retrieved from http://publications.iom.int/bookstore/free/MRS-31_EN.pdf. Visited 14.09.2013.

Castles, S., & M. Miller. (2009). *The Age of Migration. International Population Movements in the Modern World.* London – New York: Palgrave Macmillan.

Cattaneo, C., Fiorio, C., & Peri, G. (2013). What Happens to the Careers of European Workers When Immigrants "Take Their Jobs"? (IZA Discussion Paper No. 7282). Bonn: Institute for the Study of Labor (IZA). Retrieved from http://www.iza.org/en/webcontent/publications/papers/viewAbstract?dp_id=7282. Visited 14.09.2013.

CEDEFOP. (2012). *Future skills supply and demand in Europe. Forecast 2012.* Luxembourg: Publications Office of the European Union.

De Haas, H. (2008). Migration and development. A theoretical perspective. (Working Paper 9). International Migration Institute, James Martin 21st Century School, University of Oxford, 2008.

De Haas, H. (2010). Migration transitions: a theoretical and empirical inquiry into the developmental drivers of international migration. (Working Paper 24). International Migration Institute, James Martin 21st Century School, University of Oxford. Retrieved from http://www.imi.ox.ac.uk/pdfs/imi-working-papers/wp24-migration-transitions-1. Visited 14.09.2013.

Delgado, R., Márquez, H., & Rodríguez, H. (2009). Six Theses to Demystify the Nexus Between Migration And Development. *Migración y Desarrollo*. 12, 27–49.

Eurobarometer. (2010).*Eurobarometer 71. Future of Europe*. European Commission: Directorate-General for Communication.

European Commission. (2004). Directive 2004/38/EC on the Right of Union citizens and their family members to move and reside freely within the territory of the Member States.

European Commission. (2007). Regulation (EC) No 862/2007 of the European Parliament and of the Council of 11 July 2007 on Community statistics on migration and international protection and repealing Council Regulation (EEC) No 311/76 on the compilation of statistics on foreign workers.

European Commission. (2011). COM(2011) 743 final. Communication from the Commission to the European Parliament, the Council, the European Economic And Social Committee and the Committee Of The Regions: The Global Approach to Migration and Mobility.

European Commission (2013). COM(2013) 292 final. Communication from the Commission to the European Parliament, the Council, the European Economic And Social Committee and the Committee Of The Regions: Maximising the Development Impact of Migration.

Feller, E. (2004). Speech on "Are Refugees Migrants? A Dangerous Confusion." Delivered at UNHCR SID lecture "Migration and Development: Challenges for a World on the Move." Amsterdam, 27.01.2004. Retrieved from http://www.refworld.org/docid/403603a24.html. Visited 14.09.2013.

Glick Schiller, N., & Fouron. G. (2001). *Georges Woke Up Laughing: Long-Distance Nationalism and the Search for Home*. Durham, NC: Duke University Press.

Gödri, I., Soltész, B., & Bodacz, B. (2014). Immigration or emigration country? Migration trends and their socio-economic background in Hungary: A longer-term historical perspective. (Working Papers on Population, Family and Welfare, No. 19). Budapest: Hungarian Demographic Research Institute.

Hollifield, J. (2006). Migration, Trade and the Nation-State. The Myth of Globalization. In A. Messina & G. Lahav, *The Migration Reader. Exploring Politics and Policies* (pp. 170–198). London – Boulder: Lynne Rienner.

Inglehart, R., & Baker, W. (2000). Modernization, Cultural Change, and the Persistence of Traditional Values. *American Sociological Review*. 65(1), 19–51.

Joppke, Ch. (2005). *Selecting by Origin. Ethnic Migration in the Liberal State*. Cambridge, Mass. and London: Harvard University Press.

Kymlicka, W. (1995). *Multicultural Citizenship: A Liberal Theory of Minority Rights*. Oxford: Clarendon.

Labour mobility in the EU in the context of enlargement and the functioning of the transitional arrangements (2009) Final report, carried out on behalf of the Employment, Social Affairs and Equal Opportunities Directorate General of the European Commission (contract VC/2007/0293). Retrieved from http://ec.europa.eu/social/keyDocuments.jsp?type=0&policyArea=0&subCategory=0&country=0&year=2009&advSearchKey=transitional+arrangements&mode=advancedSubmit&langId=en. Visited 14.09.2013.

Levitt, P. (2001). *The transnational villagers.* Berkeley: University of California Press.

Light, I. (1972). *Ethnic Enterprise in America.* Berkeley: University of California Press.

Martin, P., & Taylor, E. (1996). The anatomy of a migration hump. In J. Taylor, *Development strategy, employment, and migration: Insights from models* (pp. 43–62). Paris: Organisation for Economic Co-operation and Development.

Massey, D., Arango, J., Hugo, G., Kouaouci, A., Pellegrino, A., & Taylor, E. (1993). Theories of International Migration: A Review and Appraisal. *Population and Development Review.* 19(3), 431–466.

McEwen, N. (2002). State Welfare Nationalism: The Territorial Impact of Welfare State Development in Scotland. *Regional & Federal Studies.* 12(1), 66–90.

Meer, N., & Noorani, T. (2008). A sociological comparison of anti-Semitism and anti-Muslim sentiment in Britain. *The Sociological Review.* 56(2), 195–219.

Melegh, A. (2006). *On the East-West Slope: Globalization, Nationalism, Racism and Discourses on Eastern Europe.* Budapest: Central European University Press.

Melegh, A. (2012). Net Migration and Historical Development in Southeastern Europe since 1950. *Hungarian Historical Review.* 1(3-4), 415–453.

Migration and Remittances Factbook (2011). The World Bank.

Orozco, M. (2005). Transnationalism and Development: Trends and Opportunities in Latin America. In S. Maimbo & D. Ratha, *Remittances: Development Impact and Future Prospects* (pp. 307–329). The World Bank.

Paoletti, E. (2010). Deportation, non-deportability and ideas of membership. (Working Paper Series No. 65). Refugee Studies Centre, Oxford Department of International Development, University of Oxford. Retrieved from http://www.rsc.ox.ac.uk/publications/deportation-non-deportability-and-ideas-of-membership Visited 14.09.2013.

Poulain, M., & Herm, A. (2010). Population Stocks Relevant to International Migration. (Working Paper No. 11, Promoting Comparative Quantitative Project (PROMINSTAT)). Retrieved from http://www.prominstat.eu/drupal/?q=system/files/Working+Paper+11+Stocks.pdf. Visited 14.09.2013.

Said, E. (1977). *Orientalism.* London: Penguin.

Sardinha, J. (2009). *Immigrant Associations, Integration and Identity: Angolan, Brazilian and Eastern European Communities in Portugal.* Amsterdam: Amsterdam University Press.

Sassen, S. (1999). *Guests and Aliens.* New York: The New Press.

Sassen, S. (2006). Foreign Investment: A Neglected Variable. In A. Messina & G. Lahav, *The Migration Reader. Exploring Politics and Policies* (pp. 596–608). London – Boulder: Lynne Rienner.

Schierup, C., Hansen, P., & Castles, S. (2006). *Migration, Citizenship and the European Welfare State. A European Dilemma.* Oxford: Oxford University Press.

Sørensen, N. N. (2004). *The Development Dimension of Migrant Remittances.* (Migration Policy Research Working Paper Series No. 1). Geneva: International Organization for Migration.

Stolcke, V. (1995). Talking Culture: New Boundaries, New Rhetorics of Exclusion in Europe. *Current Anthropology.* 36(1), 1 –24.

Sumption, M. (2013). *Tackling Brain Waste: Strategies to Improve the Recognition of Immigrants' Foreign Qualifications.* Washington, DC: Migration Policy Institute.

United Nations. (1951). *Convention relating to the Status of Refugees.*

United Nations. (1980). *Convention on the Protection of the Rights of All Migrant Workers and Members of Their Families.*

United Nations. (1998). *Recommendations on Statistics of International Migration, Rev. 1.*

Vertovec, S. (2002). Islamophobia and Muslim Recognition in Britain. In Y. Haddad, *Muslims in the West: From Sojourners to Citizens* (pp. 32–33). Oxford, New York: Oxford University Press.

Wallerstein, I. (1979). *The capitalist world-economy.* Cambridge: Cambridge University Press.

Wolff, L. (1994). *Inventing Eastern Europe: The Map of Civilization on the Mind of the Enlightenment.* Redwood City, CA: Stanford University Press.

World Bank. (2010): Bilateral Migration Matrix. Retrieved from http://econ.worldbank.org/ WBSITE/EXTERNAL/EXTDEC/EXTDECPROSPECTS/0,,contentMDK:228031 31~pagePK:64165401~piPK:64165026~theSitePK:476883,00.html. Visited 14.09.2013.

Zhou, M. (2004). Revisiting Ethnic Entrepreneurship: Convergences, Controversies, and Conceptual Advancements. *International Migration Review.* 38(3), 1040–1074.

Zincone, G., & Caponio, T. (2006). The Multilevel Governance of Migration. In R. Penninx, M. Berger & K. Kraal, *The Dynamics of International Migration and Settlement in Europe. A State of the Art* (pp. 269–304.). Amsterdam: Amsterdam University Press.

NOTES ON CONTRIBUTORS

Péter Balázs, PhD. is professor and Jean Monnet Ad Personem Chair at the Department of International Relations and European Studies, Central European University, Budapest. His research activities are centered on the foreign policy of the European Union and on problems of modernization and integration of the Eastern part of the continent. He also researches questions of European governance, including the future of European institutions. Pr. Balázs heads the Center for EU Enlargement Studies at CEU, combining his experience as a trained diplomat with academic research.

András Deák, PhD. is Senior Research Fellow at the Institute of World Economics, Hungarian Academy of Sciences, Budapest. He received his Diploma (MA) and his Doctorate (PhD) in International Relations in 1997 and 2003 respectively, both from the University of Economic Sciences, Hungary. His research fields cover in particular economic processes in the post-Soviet space, integration into the world economy and energy policy. His activities include foreign and energy policy analysis, political and corporate consultancy on Hungarian energy issues, and civilian activities in the field of energy conservation.

András Rácz, PhD. is Senior Research Fellow at The Finnish Institute of International Affairs (FIIA) in Helsinki. A specialist on issues of Russian and post-Soviet security policy, he defended his PhD in Modern History at the Eötvös Loránd University in Budapest in 2008. Until 2014 he worked at the Hungarian Institute of International Affairs and was Assistant Professor at the Pázmány Péter Catholic University. He has been a member of the European Foreign and Security Policy Studies program (EFSPS) of the Volkswagen Foundation, and a Visiting Fellow at the Transatlantic Academy of the German Marshall Fund in Washington D.C.

Béla Soltész is a junior researcher currently working at the Hungarian Central Statistical Office, Budapest, as deputy project manager of the SEEMIG research project on migration in Southeast Europe, and a PhD candidate in International Relations at Corvinus University, Budapest. His research focuses on migration and diaspora policies for development, with a special interest in comparing Latin America (especially Mexico) and Eastern Europe in terms of migratory patterns and processes and of their political and institutional frameworks for migration management.

András Szalai is a PhD candidate at the Political Science Department of the Central European University, Budapest, and a junior researcher at the university's Center for EU Enlargement Studies. His doctoral research focuses on the role of foreign policy experts in policy formulation, while his professional interests include European foreign and security policy, transatlantic relations and foreign policy decision making.

Katalin Varga is a PhD candidate at the Doctoral School of Political Science, Public Policy and International Relations of the Central European University, Budapest. Her research interests include financial systems and regulations, the Asian development model, and integration theories, including new regionalism. Apart from analyzing the EU's measures to integrate its neighboring countries, she is currently researching the evolution of financial regulation in selected Southeast Asian countries.